fa #82205A

THE PROMISE OF FULFILLMENT

stop waiting... start now!

By Paulette Sun Davis

Published by:
Empowerment Technology Corporation
1390 N. McDowell Blvd., Suite G-138
Petaluma, CA 94954

Library of Congress Cataloging-in-Publication Data
Davis, Paulette Sun, 1945—

ISBN 978-0-578-01645-0

For my children, Nicole and Michael,

who have given me the gift of their

unconditional love...

Table Of Contents

Acknowledgments

I am a student of life. I have had many teachers and I thank them all, including the ones, who through their example, taught me what not to do.

I want to specifically thank several people who have had a great impact on my work, and who have poked and prodded me along in my journey. My appreciation for them grows as I grow into a greater understanding.

Dr. John Thompson first introduced me to the idea of attachment. Letting go of attachment is truly a practice for life and opens up the possibility of healing relationships. We had many friendly arguments over what was the most important value, truth or love. He was on the side of truth and I was on the side of love. I have come to see truth and love as two sides of a coin as you shall find in my writing.

Dr. Peggy Bassett inspired me through her willingness to find a gift in every condition no matter how devastating. Her willingness to stand on the edge of the known and the unknown, lighting the way, gave me courage to face life's adversities and to experience the joy in each moment.

Wally Arnold demonstrates with every word an unswerving dedication to challenge the limits of my current thinking. His ability to find a possibility in the most difficult situation is refreshing and a gift.

Lloyd Tupper is simply the most generous person you can meet. His prayers and love have travelled with me for many years as an example of love in action.

Acknowledgments

I want to thank my editors, Magdalen Bowyer and Jessica Keet. Maggie was unrelenting in making sure I wrote with my authentic voice. Our many conversations informed and inspired my writing. She is truly a writer's coach. She asked questions that caused me to think deeply about my subject. Jessica's early support of the book kept me going. At the end, she was instrumental in making sure my words made sense and were grammatically correct. Although I must admit I took a few liberties and added some final words before it went to print!

And most importantly, I want to thank my husband, who is my partner in all pursuits. He is my inspiration and my love. He's that rare person who can truly look into a subject with discovery in mind. He asks questions out of curiosity, laughs at my jokes, listens, and teaches me to be still and know who I am. We've worked together for 30 years on developing models for waking up and living a fulfilled life.

I also want to thank my family and friends who read the final copy: Wally Arnold, Kathy Arnold, Michael Mercolino, Eileen Mercolino, and Rose Robles for their steadfast attention to detail. A special thank you to Margory Cohen for her illuminating feedback, and a deep gratitude to my daughter, Nicole, for pressing me on, from beginning to end, with her project management skills and her belief in the book.

I have been collecting quotes and memorable ideas for the last 20 years on scraps of paper. I have them tucked away in drawers and computer files, only to happen on them sometime later, but always at an opportune moment. It is with great hope that I have acknowledged the sources of the quotes accurately and you will be inspired as I have been. However, I am responsible for the ideas and recommendations made herein.

Introduction

"I couldn't wait for success so I went ahead without it."
Jonathan Winters

Writing a book is a solitary project that all your friends and associates know you're doing and ask, "Is it done yet?" Yes I am happy to say, it's finally complete but only because at some point I had to stop adding to a topic that you can explore for a lifetime.

I will underscore a simple and clear idea throughout this book: fulfillment is in the action you take right now. You don't have to wait until the goal is reached to be fulfilled. You don't have to wait for that difficult person to leave your organization for your life to be fulfilled. You don't have to wait for conditions to change to be fulfilled.

While taking action is essential to change your life, there is more to life and accomplishment than just doing, even when you're doing the right things. The key to fulfillment is to be found not merely in what you do, but why you are doing it and who you are growing into as you take each step.

The intention of this book is to provide you ideas and practices to consciously direct your commitment. You will find that commitment springs not from knowing how, but from a readiness to accept responsibility for your fulfillment now.

All our lives we're told that life is short so make it matter. What matters to you may be different from your parents, friends, boss, or co-workers. It may be different from what you have been led to believe brings happiness and well-being. At some point the realization may come that life is *too long* not to be fulfilled in what you do. So you begin to contemplate a journey. A course of action to access what fulfillment means to you and the difference that could make in your life, relationships, and at work today.

As you read this book you will find ways to accomplish results in areas where it has been difficult, move beyond the reasons that have stopped you and be prepared for the unexpected obstacles that often show up around a commitment to achieve something new—especially a new way of being. The ideas presented here will prepare you to identify and challenge any self-limiting stories that could keep you from ever getting started. It will challenge you to look at your relationships with people and with life itself.

When you operate from fulfillment, you'll notice differences and obstacles dropping away not by ignoring them, but by dealing with them when they first show up. Read this book with the idea in mind that you will never be the same again. It's in this spirit you will be inspired to think in new ways, as you engage with the ideas presented here and apply the practices to your personal and professional life.

This book is an opportunity for you to explore the substance and implications of your actions, not as a passive theory or concept, but as a force that impacts your life and the lives of others. I wrote this book to encourage you to venture out beyond the world with which you have become familiar and act in new, untried ways that bring a deeper fulfillment. You'll notice that you stop waiting for fulfillment to find you; instead you'll bring it to every situation, conversation, problem, conflict, job, and relationship. I will show you how.

Chapter 1

Start With Fulfillment In Mind

"What would you do if your success was assured?" Sign on Jennifer Grace's desk

Have you ever asked someone where she wanted to go for dinner and she tells you she doesn't care? And you say, "Great, let's have Chinese." And she says, "I hate Chinese, too salty." "Okay," you say, "how about Italian?" "No, I'm not eating carbs." Then you say, "Well, what do you want?" "I don't care, you choose." If this little conversation spoils your appetite, imagine going through life saying what you don't want versus what you do want. When you dare to say what you want, you have the opportunity to take action to move you forward, at least to the right restaurant!

It's a simple question, "What do you want?" And one that is most often answered, "I don't know!" Actually saying what you want brings you closer to finding out whether it's a fantasy or something you will achieve. Because in those moments of clarity you know that right after declaring what you want comes working for what you want.

Take a moment and imagine that what you are currently doing is exactly what you want to do. Imagine that you're doing it because it is fulfilling. It gives meaning to your life to be an entrepreneur, minister, psychologist, firefighter, police officer, pilot, CEO, spouse, mate, partner, accountant, supervisor, parent, retiree, farmer, monk, judge, lawyer, gardener, retailer, student, realtor, executive, yogi, line worker, painter, builder or volunteer ... you fill in the blank.

If you're thinking, *I'm only doing this because I have to*, or *I've been doing this for so long, what else would I do?* Stop and ask yourself if you didn't do it, then what? What's the consequence of choosing something different from the status quo? And what is it costing you to continue this way?

If you're not fulfilled, ask yourself what you are making more important than being fulfilled. Whatever your first answer is (making money, family obligations, years invested, etc.) continue the inquiry by asking yourself if your first answer wasn't the only issue, what would it be?

This is a deeper inquiry where you can contemplate both who you are and what you do at work, in relationships, or in life. Fulfillment is the practice of reuniting who you are with what you do.

Do you have the freedom to choose what you want? There comes a point in your life where the ability to choose something different from what you are doing now, or what other people want you to do, is both freeing and frightening. It's freeing because you take accountability for your happiness. It's frightening ... well, for the same reason. You get to own your decisions, set new goals, make mistakes, and have a direct experience of life. You find out what you can do, how creative and resourceful you are, and you stop waiting for fulfillment to find you. Being fulfilled is a conscious choice. When you make that choice, it opens a door to what's possible.

One way to approach fulfillment is to talk to a valued friend who can ask you questions about what you're doing and why; someone who's interested in your happiness. I have some special coaches who I talk to when I'm taking on a big goal or have an important decision to make. I don't just talk to anybody, only to someone who is a committed listener, who thinks outside the constraints of current conditions and can freely have a conversation about possibilities. I want someone who can imagine with me, but who doesn't automatically agree with me. I'm not looking for someone to tell me what to do, or to agree or disagree; but to listen, ask questions, and offer insight. It's this process that helps me clarify purpose and direction.

At the end of the day, no matter how much coaching you get, you're the one who chooses the goal, the relationship, the role, the job, the conversation, and you create the experience of fulfillment.

Start with fulfillment in mind. When you answer the question "What do you want?" stop and ask yourself "What will this choice fulfill?" The experience of fulfillment is in each action you take right now. This idea came to me as I noticed what I was thinking about when I woke up one morning. I noticed that my thoughts were tied to an evaluation of what happened the day before. This only occurred when what I did the day before, the choices I made, weren't fulfilling and weren't in alignment with my goals or what I said I wanted. I noticed that this was a recurring experience. I'd wake up and evaluate my actions from the previous day, covering anything from work, eating, exercising, money, time, or conversations and say, "Why did I do that?" When there was no trace of yesterday, I noticed I woke up refreshed, present, and ready for the new day.

I started thinking about a practice that would have me consciously create fulfillment in the moment of taking action, versus reacting or compensating for what I did or didn't do.

And then it occurred to me.

Fulfillment is in the action I'm taking right now. Not in the action I will take, not in the action I should've taken, but in the action I take right now!

For me it's slowing down in the moment to ask myself "Will this action sustain fulfillment at least through waking up tomorrow?"

Just until tomorrow. It's not a long time. Just 24 hours. It slows me down long enough to consider fulfillment in both of its meanings: 1) being fulfilled and 2) achieving an intended result. When you're operating with fulfillment in mind, it's sustainable. You enjoy the moment, make the best decisions based on the information you have, and sow no seeds of disappointment. It's also important to understand that operating from fulfillment includes making mistakes. Mistakes and breakdowns are part of living a fulfilled life. That's how we grow in our achievements and abilities.

Practice: *Just for today, slow down your actions to consider why you are doing what you're doing before you do it, including the possibility of taking no action in the moment.*

This practice can be as simple as repeating this mantra—"Fulfillment is in the action I'm taking right now"—until it becomes part of your inner guidance, allowing you to consider what you want to achieve and why. This internal declaration will bring you present so you can connect to your choice in the making. This practice increases your awareness and gets you in front of the choices you are about to make. It will slow you down to think through what you want and begin the process of awakening fulfillment by making deliberate choices.

Chapter 2

Fulfillment Or Disappointment?

"I went to the woods to learn to live deliberately, to confront only the essential facts of life, and see if I could not learn what they had to teach, and not, when I came to die, discover that I had not lived."
Henry David Thoreau

You may find that you're fulfilled in some areas of your life and disappointed in others. It helps to keep in mind that you are not looking for perfection, just progress. However progress is not automatic. Continued disappointment can be a vehicle to notice a pattern that could reveal where you are stuck and not making any progress.

If you're going to act in new ways to achieve something unprecedented and be fulfilled along the way, something must change in how you manage your life and commitments day to day. This requires the recognition that you must start where you are because in fact you can't start anywhere else! The moment has come to look in the mirror of self-reflection and take a deep breath and say, "OK, let's look." I say the plural 'let's look,' because you're looking with your whole body, heart, and mind. What are you looking into? You're looking into what ignites your passion. You're looking into where you are in your life … job, health, relationships, joy, love, family, and what you are thinking and saying about your life right now.

If you're reading this book, you are probably at a point of change. You may be curious about what's possible. You may be reassessing what's meaningful to you in your life. You may be getting signals that something's missing. I've heard people call it a "crisis in confidence" or a "mid-life crisis" or a "stop the world, I want to get off" moment. It can be the recognition that you'll be working longer than you thought so you think about shifting your course to an unrealized dream. It can be a persistent inner voice or a growing awareness calling you to wake up now.

As you begin to look, you may start noticing what you value and believe is possible. You start discovering what you bring to every activity, job, relationship, conversation, and choice. Is what you bring fulfillment, full engagement, and commitment?

Fulfillment starts with a vision, not just the enthusiasm that most people have at the beginning of something; it's a sustainable vision that moves you into consistent action. It's a lining up of who you are and what you do. There's not a separate you going about your business when you operate from fulfillment. You're not doing something and complaining about it. Instead you disappear into the action. Fulfillment is the framework you look through, the context, from start to finish. You realize moment to moment that you're exercising, dieting, investing, saving, studying, working, thinking, changing, volunteering, creating … because you want to. It's not a have to; it's what you choose to do. There's no separation between who you are and what you're doing.

You may struggle along the way and find you struggle more in making a choice to do what's fulfilling than in taking the action itself. Once you make the choice the struggle ends. I experience this almost daily in getting up to exercise. Once I'm running or doing yoga there's no struggle. The struggle is in deciding to just do it. Fulfillment is infused with focus. What you focus on prospers. Take that idea to heart. It's the law of attraction in action.

You start with a vision of what's possible and know the action comes out of a bold but often simple plan to take one step at a time, one moment at a time, because ... really ... the only moment is now.

George Bernard Shaw wrote that "People are always blaming their circumstances for what they are. I don't believe in circumstances. The people who get on in this world are the people who get up and look for the circumstances they want, and if they can't find them, make them."

That kind of thinking allows you to envision what you want to achieve and not be stopped before you get started by what's required to get it done. Stop for a minute and think about how you have achieved anything. You'd most likely tell me in some way that you had a vision of what was possible, you took action, and completed what you set out to do. I call this the cycle of fulfillment.

As you review this cycle the impact of what you say and do moment to moment will become clear and inform what moves you toward or away from what you want to achieve.

Just as importantly you will become aware of the choices you make that can stop you. You'll become aware of how those choices can actually reverse your direction away from being fulfilled and away from what you say you want.

Cycle Of Fulfillment

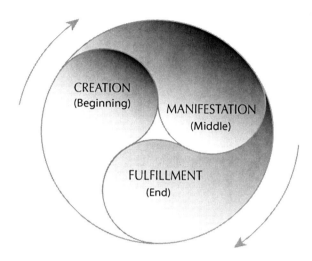

The cycle of fulfillment includes three phases: the creation phase (vision), the manifestation phase (action), and the fulfillment phase (completion).

Creation–Vision: Now imagine the cycle of fulfillment as forward-moving. To accomplish anything you start at the beginning, in creation, with an idea, a vision of what's possible. It's an experience of waking up and recognizing the contribution that is uniquely yours to make. You're not focused on limitations; you're focused on your vision of a life worth living. It's a way to connect with something that gives meaning to your life and brings your focus present to this moment. Your vision guides and organizes your actions. Your vision shapes the choices you make. Once you've committed to a vision, which is no small task, it's yours. This is true whether it's your creation or you join a team where the vision is already formed. If you don't own the vision of the team or the organization, you'll go through the motions every day to do a job, but fulfillment will be missing for you. The creation phase is critical. It's here where you envision and declare not only the goal but also your success. You start with the end in mind.

Manifestation–Action: From this powerful beginning you move into manifestation, which is the middle of the cycle. That's where you share the vision, generate agreement and make detailed plans, take action, and deal with obstacles and the reality of accomplishing a goal. Giving up is not an option. You may change your strategy to achieve fulfillment but you don't stop. You achieve the goal and you get what you aimed for and everything that goes along with it including obstacles and unimaginable success. So plan with attention and care. Deal with obstacles and conflict when they first arise, correct and learn from mistakes, and ask for help before you need it.

Fulfillment–Completion: Achievement comes, which is the final part of the cycle, where you do what it takes to be complete and satisfied. Being fulfilled travels with you throughout the cycle. You probably will be dissatisfied from time to time or have failures along the way and, in the cycle of fulfillment, they don't stop you or derail the goal. They inform new action. And the action transforms you. You learn and self-correct. You accept feedback and acknowledge yourself and others for a job well done. There's a difference between information that fuels a solution and explanations that excuse inaction. Feedback is part of completion and transforms criticism into valuable information. What you did worked or didn't work. If it didn't work you make a course correction. There is power in completion. You only have to look at anything you've put off doing and then finished it to experience the power of completion. You'll notice you have more energy when you complete tasks and goals. Completion transforms you.

Why don't people complete what they start? I've asked thousands of people why they didn't finish the final phase and many tell me it's because they encountered a problem and stopped.

Instead of giving up, what's essential is to stay open to feedback. You stay open to feedback so you can self-correct along the way. This seems so obvious and yet the response we often receive when working on team projects is that when people bring feedback they don't get a big thank you. Instead they're often seen as troublemakers, naysayers, and limited thinkers. I think it's important to reverse that behavior if it exists in your organization, projects or relationships. Don't give in to the urge to defend, explain, and justify what doesn't work. Defending, explaining and justifying prevents you from listening to feedback. Listening to feedback can create breakthroughs in your thinking that fuels new solutions.

You may not act on all the feedback you get and sometimes feedback isn't easy to hear, but it's in your interest to listen and carefully consider what others tell you. You'll find that the respect you offer in listening to others will be repaid in kind. If you've ever told anyone, "I should have listened to you!" you know the power of honest feedback and a relationship founded on respect. If you build a strong background of relationship it will weather any feedback. Part of my practice and commitment is to listen to anything and ask questions. I let people know that in business and in my relationships. It opens the channel for fulfilling and effective communication.

So is it really problems or not listening to feedback that prevents completion, or could it be that a compelling vision is missing?

Let's go back to the beginning. Some people are great at beginnings but then stop. Why? Some years ago my husband and I ran a process with over two hundred people looking at this cycle. We asked the audience to divide into three groups based on where they found themselves operating most of the time: the "vision" group (beginnings), the "action" group (middles), and the "completion" group (endings). Which group do you think was the biggest? If you said the "vision" group you'd be right—it had over 125 people. The "action" group had about 75 and the "completion" group had 5!

Beginnings

The group who loved beginnings reported that the creation phase was full of hope and enthusiasm. This group loved exploring possibilities. They reported that the enthusiasm could carry them into action for a while, but wasn't always sufficient to move them to completion. Does this sound like New Year's resolutions? The beginning is full of promise, something new, but if it doesn't move you into action it can easily become a fantasy along with a track record of false starts. And no matter how much you tell yourself that Edison found 400 ways not to make the light bulb, he was in action the whole time, working with a team, meeting obstacles head on, and not wavering from his vision. Edison was dedicated to producing an electric lamp for indoor use. Obstacles didn't stop him. Obstacles have the power to bring your focus to what needs attention now. The focus shifts from the outcome to what you need to do today so you can be fully present and engaged in the process.

22

In the beginning, you're not looking at how long it might take, or the day-to-day aggravation that might occur; instead you're creating a vision of what's possible that consistently organizes your time, focus, and action. You're not attached to the outcome; you're committed to bringing something into being.

Have you noticed that in theory everything works perfectly? You're not up against the reality of action when you're visioning. You're not up against making money, making requests for resources, generating agreement, interviewing, or risking!

Some people in this group also reported that their vision was so strong they couldn't refuse it. They had to be in action no matter how long it took to accomplish their goal. The upside of this group is they understood the power of vision. We were conducting this program for Dr. Peggy Bassett, a powerful minister and wonderful friend. She taught beginning ministers to bring a vision to their organizations and be the steward of the vision. And those that were successful, like Peggy, also understood that vision is an organizing principle that sustains action, no matter what obstacles or opposition you encounter along the way. Like Edison, if you never give up, your vision will lead you to even greater accomplishments than you might have imagined possible in the beginning.

Middles

The action group discovered that sometimes a vision was missing, which could have sustained them through the obstacles to accomplishing any goal. They also realized that they were the ones in meetings who didn't like to discuss possibilities, but would rather run out of the room and solve the problem before getting full information. These were the folks that had less time for planning and more often learned through mistakes.

Years back I was asked to talk to a company about developing a conflict resolution process. The owner of the company was there along with other members of the executive team. The conflict was between two members of management that was impacting the operations of the whole company. I asked questions and answered inquiries about what I could do to teach them a model for resolving conflict. Before 30 minutes passed the owner was on the phone calling a hotel to schedule the sessions. I had to chuckle. I didn't even have to write a proposal! I conducted the conflict resolution process and coached the owner for many years. The owner preferred immediate action and it took some time and coaching to have him plan more effectively to secure the best possible outcomes. He got a lot done and was very successful. His challenge was saying yes too fast before he considered the commitment he was making. He would have a moment of fulfillment in saying yes and then almost immediate regret. This is a common mistake for people who love action. He was constantly over-committed and his wife's continual complaint was that he didn't know how to say no! You can say no and be fulfilled. You just have to slow down.

I know personally how hard that can be for people who are biased toward action. I worked with a CFO who encouraged me to slow down. He would say, "Let's think through this action to ensure that we're making the right choices and not complicating the problem." He was a good teacher. I was always in a hurry to solve the problem right away. Then I remembered that old saying "Let's sleep on it," a helpful strategy if there's a commitment to discovery and resolution. When I "sleep on it," I often discover something I didn't see in the moment. I can also think about the impact of the solution or the impact of the commitment. Sometimes you have to act immediately, more often you don't; better planning can lead you to put the force of your action in the direction you want to go. Vision organizes your actions, planning tells you what steps to take, and commitment moves you through the obstacles. Obstacles are seen as stepping-stones along the way to fulfilling the goal.

The upside of this group is they get things done and would rather take action and learn from their mistakes than do nothing.

Endings

I was very interested in the small group that said they were most attracted to completion. They reported that they often moved too quickly to an end and were uncomfortable staying in the process of visioning or getting things done. "Let's just get through this" was their battle cry. When asked whether they were satisfied with the end, they said they didn't take the time to experience fulfillment, but rather moved on to the next thing and started over. I put this in the context of many resumes I've seen where applicants have jumped from job to job. When I asked them why they left a certain position, they reported that it didn't turn out the way they anticipated. That could be true for any of us, depending on the situation. The challenge is to notice whether "jumping" is a pattern and what that pattern tells you. It may tell you that you always think things will be better elsewhere—be it a relationship, a job, or a new location. The grass is not always greener. Sometimes you jump from an ending into something new and experience spinning your wheels. You know the old saying "Everywhere you go there you are!" You're the consistent piece of the formula. Instead of action that moves you forward to accomplish what you say you want, it can move you into an endless string of activities, which fill up your time and your life, but may not fulfill you.

The upside of this group is bringing a goal to completion and making sure they know what it takes to be complete. They're not happy unless they're checking things off their list! This group was asked to reflect on what they were committed to when they wanted to get to completion at all costs. Their answers were insightful. Control was an issue. Checking things off their list gave them the "feeling" of being in control and also gave them a momentary sense of fulfillment. Being out of control meant they had to look inside and be fulfilled in the space of "no doing". They had to confront being patient with those who had other priorities.

I noticed this when I was moving a divisional office from the west coast to the east coast and only a few people were going to make the transition to the "snowy" side of the country. One member of the team got increasingly more productive at the end. She was a whirlwind of activity making sure everything got done ahead of schedule whether it was her job or just needed to be done. On the surface we were all grateful for what she did to bring the transition to a successful completion. When I looked a little deeper into "who" she was, as she did the tasks, I quickly realized it was her way of masking her sadness at this ending and covering up a feeling of being "out of control". To avoid the sadness and emptiness of not having something to do she just rushed through getting everything done, checking tasks off her list at lightning speed. When we sat down and talked about it, she just cried, "Will I ever see these people again?" "Of course, if you want to," I told her. For her it was a little like a death. She was still letting go and accepting endings as part of the cycle of fulfillment. Some of the staff started a weekly get-together where they could meet, say hello and find out what each person was up to. It became a treasured time to stay connected. Pretty soon folks who had left the organization years earlier started to attend. An ending doesn't mean a break in the connection. We're all connected in physical, psychological, and spiritual ways.

Practice: *Reflect on how you operate in beginnings, middles, and endings, and the difference between those that are fulfilling or disappointing to you.*

What do you tell yourself and how does that impact the actions you take?

In the areas where you're not complete, what stops you from completing what you set out to do? For now, just notice.

Chapter 3

The Beginning, Middle, And End

"Someone's sitting in the shade today because someone planted a tree a long time ago." Warren Buffet

Creation:
Powerful Beginnings

Imagine that you are at the beginning of setting a goal. The first thing you do is come up with an idea of what you want to accomplish, knowing that your idea fulfills something. It fulfills a vision of what's possible and meaningful for you. Powerful goals start with fulfillment in mind.

You can access fulfillment by looking into your vision of a life worth living. What ignites your passion? If you want your work to be fulfilling, it must fit into your overall vision. I chuckled when I read a recruiting ad that instructed readers to think about what they'd do for free. The ad said that once you know what you'd do for free, find a job that pays you for that role. That's starting with fulfillment in mind.

The declaration of your vision in the creation phase of the cycle of fulfillment is powerful. It requires ownership, commitment, and accountability to do what it takes. When that ownership is missing ask yourself whether the vision and goals are your idea of fulfillment, or someone else's idea of fulfillment. Take a breath and simply ask yourself "What is my vision of a life worth living?" There could be immediate responses or perhaps silence. It's not a question that most people ask themselves. The practice is to sit with the question and allow what's authentic to percolate, and come to the surface.

In the creation phase you want to focus on what's possible. In fact, if you consider how you are going to do something too soon, you shut down the creative process and can't even consider something you don't already know how to accomplish. All you have to do is watch how management teams interact to observe the conflict between those that want to get down to business and those that want to explore what's possible. This can be an area of contention between the folks that want to get to the "how" before the team has uncovered emerging ideas, possibilities, and discoveries that happen when you stay in a "visioning" conversation longer than everyone is comfortable. This is as true in personal relationships as it is on management teams.

In the creation phase you ask yourself these kinds of questions:

What do I want to accomplish?
What's possible?
What gives my life meaning?
What areas need to improve?
What do I want to change?
What matters most?

Allow yourself to inquire without negating any response. Give yourself time to discover your vision and look into what's possible. Then you can sort through those possibilities. Once you have the vision, and feel the pull of commitment, goals become clear and the "how" gets designed. Vision comes first.

Next comes a structure for fulfillment.

Let me give you a commonly shared example of how vision and commitment come first. It's about how Roger Bannister broke the four-minute mile. In the early 1950s the human body paradigm—the prevailing thinking at that time with all the resulting rules and regulations governing the human body—determined that it was physiologically impossible for a human body to run a mile in less than four minutes. Roger Bannister was a medical student at the time. He questioned that paradigm and committed to breaking what he thought was a limited notion. When he described the psychological impact of the four-minute barrier in an interview with *Forbes*, he related the following, "The world record then was four minutes, 1.4 seconds, held by Sweden's Gunder Haegg. It had been stuck there for nine years. It didn't seem logical to me, as a physiologist/doctor, that if you could run a mile in four minutes, one-and-a-bit seconds, you couldn't break four minutes. But it had become a psychological as well as a physical barrier."

Once the breakthrough happens we often think it's obvious because we now have the evidence. Think about not having any evidence only the power to question and challenge what we think we know! That's the power of vision.

The vision came first. Then Bannister figured out how to do it. He teamed up with other runners who were also committed to breaking the four-minute mile. They decided the best way to accomplish the goal was not to race against each other, but to support Bannister by pacing his laps when he ran the race. He ran a three-minute 59.4-second mile. Not only did he shave time off the previous world record, the evidence that it couldn't be done collapsed. Most people wait to see evidence before they believe something is possible. His vision and commitment came first. The power of his shared vision and commitment produced a breakthrough. Not only could he break the four-minute barrier, other people started breaking it too. Only six weeks later the record was broken again.

You probably know people who will take steps to accomplish a new goal and then stop before they complete what they set out to do. They take some action and don't get the desired result, then use it as an opportunity to reaffirm a limiting belief and end up with a story that says, "I knew it couldn't be done."

Barriers and obstacles are part of the process. They challenge you. They challenge your current ability. They challenge your current body of knowledge and they challenge your resourcefulness.

What you currently do is in service to something. What is that something? What is the vision that is organizing your actions today?

This may begin some deep soul searching on your part to discover who you are in what you do. Stay in the creation phase in the cycle of fulfillment, until you come to a point where you recognize that fulfillment comes naturally when you live your vision. If not, what you do is out of alignment with who you are.

When you sign off on a new goal make sure it connects with what is important to you. Then there is true ownership and an unswerving commitment. Once the vision is declared and the goal is set, it pulls you forward and moves you from the beginning into the middle.

Manifestation:
The Rubber Meets The Road – Middles

The next phase in the cycle of fulfillment is manifestation. The question now shifts from what to how. How are you going to get this done? What are the steps? What is the plan? The plan includes the detailed actions you will take, including sharing the vision, generating agreement, gathering resources, and identifying the milestones along the way ... those recognizable points of achievement as you move toward accomplishing your goal. The successful plan includes time frames so you can manage your commitments.

Your commitment has to be bigger than excuses and conditions. Conditions like sleeping in, watching TV, not enough time, no agreement for your ideas, and all the excuses we give ourselves when we just don't feel like it. It may require some sacrifice on your part. The journey is the commitment that transcends conditions, circumstances, and excuses. On the way to fulfillment, be fulfilled. The excuses will disappear. Then you are ready to accomplish your goal in thought (you see it done) and in action (you do it).

Sounds easy, doesn't it? Like the Nike commercial says, "Just do it!" When your vision of a life worth living organizes your actions, it is easier to get into action and stay in action. Nonetheless, it requires practice, training, and commitment to stay in action; until, one day, an outer commitment is no longer necessary. You disappear into the action and become the practice. Your commitment expands to include and deal with current conditions, instead of you being stopped by them.

We've been told many times that the journey of a thousand miles begins with the first step. This is one of those common and profound truths. It's how you develop expertise in any area. You take that first step, and then continue one step at a time, and one day you are the embodiment of what you set out to do. When that day comes, the beginning of enlightenment comes. Before enlightenment, chop wood and carry water. After enlightenment, chop wood and carry water. Take this notion to heart as you consider the achievement of any goal. If losing weight is the goal, before enlightenment, portion control and exercise. After enlightenment, it's still portion control and exercise. If getting out of debt is the goal, before enlightenment, live within your means. After enlightenment, live within your means.

The manifestation phase is critical to your success because it demands action and prepares you for obstacles. The beauty of manifestation becomes apparent when it turns into a practice, a way of being—an awakening. You only commit to what you will do. You are your word and your deeds become known in the world. It's a sacred contract. When you speak, people listen, because they know you'll do what you say. They know who you are. When you take the action to fulfill the goal and overcome the obstacles along the way, you cross over from manifestation into the ending phase of fulfillment.

Fulfillment:
The Power Of Completion – Endings

The ending in the cycle of fulfillment naturally focuses you on completion. This ending phase has two parts—completion and satisfaction. In other words the goal is fulfilled and you are fulfilled. You ask yourself, "Am I complete? Am I satisfied?" Completion includes review, acknowledgment, feedback, and lessons learned.

Sometimes people come to me feeling at a loss as they try to rekindle a dream or create a vision of a life worth living— they want to take the necessary steps to move into the cycle of fulfillment but they don't feel particularly creative. When this happens, I start by asking the question "What's incomplete?" Sometimes we're so filled up with what's incomplete there's no room to explore what's new.

What's incomplete holds your focus in the past. Whatever is on your list is only incomplete because you made a promise to yourself or another person that was never fulfilled or resolved. When you make a list of what's incomplete and examine it, you'll find that some items get crossed off the list because you really don't intend to do those things anymore and perhaps you never intended to in the beginning. Perhaps you said yes in the enthusiasm of the moment without careful consideration of the impact on your other, existing commitments. Perhaps you said yes to please someone else so you didn't have to confront the truth with a "no". In order to be complete you tell the truth now and revoke your promise.

Some items on the list, you may still intend to do. You wanted to do them then and you want to do them now. You move the "want" to a commitment by taking action in a given time frame. This time you complete the action on schedule, and you don't stop until you're done. These tasks can be everything from cleaning the garage to having difficult conversations.

Fulfillment is in the action you take right now. When you carry what's incomplete around in your head, you create mental traffic that can interrupt your focus on what you've committed to today.

Fulfillment is not pretending that you're complete when

you're not. The way you'll know you're complete is you'll stop talking to yourself about it. Notice where you're incomplete and where it stops you from moving forward. There may be a few things on your list that stay on your list because you still have an intention to take action. If they stay on your list, create a timeline to complete them. Set up a time and action plan that makes sense and moves your intention to fulfillment. Examine the vision that holds these intentions in place. Then make a list of what's incomplete at work, at home, and in your relationships.

As you make this list, take a moment and think about your vision of a life worth living.

Vision Organizes Action

If your vision is organizing your actions then what is incomplete today will move to completion as part of your stated goals in the cycle of fulfillment.

Ask yourself if you are being who you are authentically, through all the stages of the cycle of fulfillment: vision, action and completion. If not, completion will seem like a "have-to" and you'll go through the motions and even complete many goals without experiencing being awake and fulfilled moment to moment. Completion is a process that can awaken a new beginning.

Ignite Your Passion

Remember these questions when you are in the beginning phase of the cycle of fulfillment:

What's possible?
What's my vision of a life worth living?
What ignites my passion?

The answers create your vision, your intention, and your goals. You ask these questions so you can be confident that setting the goal, in the first place, serves your highest good; and if the goal is at work, you include the interest of the organization, the highest good for all concerned. When you come to the ending phase of fulfillment, you can check to see whether the end matched what was aimed for in the beginning.

The ending phase may be the time to offer not only acknowledgment but also apologies. Especially in the area of challenging goals, you may find you have stepped on some toes in order to get something done. This may be the time to acknowledge people for putting up with your determination and concentration to achieve the goal, or to thank them for their assistance, and, if needed, a time to make any necessary amends. A genuine focus on relationships lets people know that you care about them and the contribution they made, as well as caring about the goal. You'll have the opportunity to build a team you can play with again. With every fulfillment comes a result—you either achieved it or you learned something critical that can move you more powerfully into creation armed with greater knowledge, experience, and insight ... a new beginning.

What's required in the cycle of fulfillment is a healthy state of detachment so you can enjoy the fruits of your labor and the lessons learned without an exaggerated sense of self-importance when you win, or of self-defeat if it didn't turn out the way you wanted. You can learn to be a highly involved participant without the attachment that occurs when one fears how what happens could reflect on their image, abilities, and future prospects.

Attachment to an outcome can keep you unnecessarily anchored in a fear of loss and can stop the natural process of fulfillment. Observe your attachment and let it go. You don't need it. Let your commitment guide you. I'll talk more about recognizing and letting go of attachment and how it undermines fulfillment in Chapter 9.

The cycle of fulfillment begins with a vision of what's possible; this organizes your actions, leaving you with the balance that comes from achieving results and living an intentional and meaningful life.

Practice: *Make a practice of being complete today. It's simple. Fulfill what you say you will do. At the end of each day, say, "I am complete for today." In this way completion becomes a process, not just an event.*

Schedule any incompletion and get it done or tell yourself (or anyone else involved) the truth that you're not going to do it in the time frame required. In that way you focus on what you want to achieve, and what you focus on prospers. You build a practice of being your word and fulfilling what you say you will do.

The result of this practice is a good night's sleep!

Chapter 4

Moving Forward Or Moving Backward

"One ship drives east and another drives west with the selfsame winds that blow. Tis the set of the sails, and not the gales, that tell us the way to go." Ella Wheeler Wilcox

If you decide that every obstacle is an indication to postpone living your vision or to change your goal, you're not operating in a cycle of fulfillment. How do you know the difference between what you really are no longer interested in doing, and something that is a block to overcome? The difference is recognizing what stops you. And more often than not, you'll find that what stops you are excuses.

Do you ever find yourself waiting for the time and space to do what fulfills you? You might be saying, "When I just have the money, relationship, or job, then I'll be fulfilled." Why are you waiting? Space and time are essential. You may say that your space and time are filled with work or other pressing responsibilities. And yet when you do have time, how do you spend it? Being out of synch with time and space is the result of not paying attention to what fulfills you.

Time and space are two fundamental ways we interact with the world, and most of us would agree we don't have enough of either. Let's consider "space" first. We'll say the space in our day is filled with work, leaving us little time to devote to our families, health, or personal interests. And yet when we do have space, many of us use it in ways that leave us unfulfilled. Space fills up when you carry around too many unresolved problems or unrealized dreams.

What would you say in response to the question "How do you fill up the space you have?" At the end of the day, does it leave you with a delicious sigh of fulfillment or a sense of longing for what you only dream about? How do you create some space in your thinking so you can actually consider something new and connect to your vision of what's possible?

What do you say about "time"? Time drags when you live too much in the past or future. Time becomes a pressure when you realize you've made more agreements than you can deliver. Agreements live in time. Agreements are commitments that spell out what you or others will do in a given time frame. This is just as true if the agreement is with yourself. Do you ever find yourself saying, "I just ran out of time," as the reason for not doing what you wanted or agreed to do? The usual way we give ourselves more time is to say, "I'll do it later." As a friend reminded me, everyone's favorite diet is the one that starts tomorrow!

Being out of synch with time is the result of not paying attention to what you say yes to each and every day.

You only have to think about what you said yes to recently, that ended up not being fulfilling, to understand the impact of not saying no in the first place. You think you'll change later, when you have time to focus on what you want, even though your instincts are to say no right now. What would it take for you to say no in the beginning rather than after you've already made the commitment?

When you realize that fulfillment is up to you to create, you stop waiting and find out what you need to start now. Otherwise fulfillment is a fantasy that you wish could come true. Fantasies are free. Fulfillment comes with a price. What's the price you're willing to pay? It will include commitment, planning, and the sacrifice of excuses.

I notice that when I use the excuse of "not enough time" I have evidence to support that notion. I'm busy! But, the truth is, I can make time with careful planning. I can get up earlier to exercise or read the paper less and write more. I'm never dissatisfied because I got up earlier to exercise or put down the paper to write, because both of those actions are part of my vision of a life worth living. My husband and I joke about this state of ecstatic fulfillment after we run, meditate, work, or do yoga noticing that we never question why we did that after any action that is fulfilling our vision; and that includes going to the gym!

There's an easy way to recognize excuses. You'll notice that you keep talking to yourself (and others) about how hard it is to achieve what you want. If you pay attention, you will hear yourself telling limiting "stories"—the kind you tell when you make a decision to stop moving forward. See whether you recognize any of these self-limiting stories, also known as excuses. Feel free to add any others to the list.

"It's too hard."
"I have too many other things to do."
"I ran out of time."
"I didn't plan it right."
"I changed my mind."
"I knew it wouldn't work!"
"I'm too tired."

"It's too late."
"I don't have enough money."
"I can't do that!"
"I'll start tomorrow" or it's cousin, "I'll do it later."
"If only I'd started earlier."
"I'm just too lazy."
"I'm too old."
"It's not in the cards."
"I don't have the education."
"I don't have the energy."

We also have stories about why we don't ask for help when we need it or make requests.

"They don't respect me."
"They don't like me."
"They'll just say no."
"I waited too long."
"No one is cooperating."
"I blew my only opportunity."
"It wasn't meant to be."
"It won't last anyway."
"Procrastination runs in my family!"
"If only I had what I needed."
"If only I had made a different choice."

These stories all point to the past. Experience tells us that we can't change the past; whatever happened, happened. Pretending that you could have done something differently has the effect of keeping you anchored in the past thinking about what you could have done, rather than considering what you could do right now.

Self-limiting stories are memories that retell your interpretation of past events. If you're telling a self-limiting story now, you may be bumping up against a boundary that stops you from seeing things as they are today. The good news is that if you're telling a limiting story, even if you have evidence to support it, it can only be true up until now and it's only true because you continue to tell the story.

Think about the story "Procrastination runs in my family!" This is a story a close friend told me recently as the reason why some things in the "Smith" family never get done. We both laughed out loud when the story poured out, and at the same time knew that it had the ring of a self-fulfilling prophecy. If you don't challenge these self-limiting stories, they can and do have the tendency to become the fallback reason why you don't do what you say you want. You have the opportunity to turn a limiting story into a portal for action when you realize that these kinds of stories are patterns, and when seen clearly, release your energy for something new. Patterns are habits and habits can be broken. Then new, intentional habits can be formed that move you in the direction you want to go.

Why do we tell stories that seem to limit us? What's the benefit? Well, as long as we tell the story we don't have to do anything about it! It also may bring a momentary relief or balance to what didn't go our way.

I'm asking you to loosen your grip on any limiting story that you keep telling. Why? To give you some room to consider what's possible in the absence of that particular limiting story, including accepting things exactly as they are. You only have to stop bringing the "story" into this moment. When you stop you may see options that your limiting story is covering up. First, notice the limiting stories and excuses you repeatedly tell. If you have a hard time identifying these stories, ask someone who knows you well to reflect back to you what you say about moving forward. Not their opinion on what you say, but precisely your actual words. Just notice without judgment and reflect on what you discover.

In Chapter 2, we talked about a cycle of fulfillment. Now it's time to contrast it with a cycle of disappointment. Once you understand the difference between these two cycles it will be easier to recognize what has stopped you up until now and how to break through to fulfillment.

The cycle of fulfillment starts with creation. The cycle of disappointment starts with a fantasy. What's the difference between creation and fantasy?

Fantasy vs. Creation

Fantasy is a wish. You wish you could achieve the outcome and it stops there. You hope it will all work out. In creation you actually declare it will happen and there is ownership of the outcome—the kind of ownership and vision that puts you in action. With fantasy, commitment is missing; an unwavering commitment that is not based on mood or conditions or the behavior of others or even current knowledge. Remember Roger Bannister? His commitment wasn't based on the prevailing body of knowledge of the time. His commitment came out of his vision; a vision that breaking the four-minute mile was possible.

Fantasy, in the way I'm using it, is a flight of fancy, an ungrounded hope for the future. Instead of visioning, planning, and action in a forward-moving cycle, fantasy leads to a backward-moving cycle telling stories about why something can't be done, and leaves you disappointed.

Most people I know today use some kind of time management system. Most have alarms that go off to alert them when required actions and commitments are due. If you use a system, do you ever move those due dates from one day to the next? Maybe you move that really important item thinking, *Oh, I didn't get to that today, I'll move it to tomorrow.* And then you continue to move what's important from one day to the next. Or you might say, "I really need to get these small things out of the way so I can get to the important stuff." And then you don't make that important call that will actually move you toward achieving your goals. Or you don't write that report. Or you don't give that piece of feedback or make that request you need to make. So you wait, but you fill the space of waiting with a "story" that you'll get to it soon. The activity of putting it on a calendar may seem like action, but it can actually be a replacement for action.

Even with more technologically advanced systems tracking time and action, it's still a fantasy if you don't do it!

When we take action, we count on each other to be honest and committed enough to say yes and deliver on our promises ... or say no. Someone saying no to you doesn't stop you in the cycle of fulfillment; it's just a response that lets you know someone else's commitment.

The Power Of Saying No

No ... such a little word with so much meaning. People have asked me the same question for many years: How can you tell your boss no? Concern for saying no often arises around authority figures like your boss, parents, teachers, or maybe even your spouse or partner. My response to the question about your boss, is to pull out a list of the promises you've made and say, "This is what I'm committed to achieve. Has something changed? Is there something I can drop off my list or renegotiate so I can take this on?" The next predictable statement I hear is "You can't do that. You can't say that to your boss." Well how do you know that? People usually respond with a half-suppressed laugh when I ask them how they know that, but they get the point. They realize they assumed they couldn't tell the truth on the job. They couldn't say no or even have a conversation about it. And they were content to suffer instead of saying no or negotiating or telling the truth so alternatives could be explored. What they had was a limiting story about managers, and that same kind of thinking impacted any relationship where they didn't think they could say no.

Hearing "no" in the cycle of fulfillment is recognized as a legitimate, committed response. Part of your plan may be to make requests of another person, a customer, or a family member. People can say no. But a "no" in the cycle of fulfillment doesn't stop you. In fact, it could be the beginning of a negotiation or an opportunity to ask some clarifying questions and begin a dialogue or discussion to learn more. In your important relationships you begin to discover what someone really thinks and what they want. In relationships, this kind of truthfulness creates closeness because someone you care about doesn't have to hide behind an inauthentic "yes."

No is not an exit sign for your commitment or your relationship. An authentic "no" throws you into the unknown and can put you at the beginning of a true exploration of what's possible. When you're not afraid to hear someone say no, it most likely follows that you are not afraid to say no. In the cycle of fulfillment you're clear on what you are committed to do. When you're clear, and someone asks you to do something that would prevent you from keeping your existing commitments, you say no.

In the cycle of disappointment someone saying no can be heard as a reason to stop and exit the goal. So instead of looking at what you can do, you end up disappointed, focusing on self-defeating stories about how hard it is, why you can't get it done, or how nobody wants to do it.

Cycle Of Disappointment

FANTASY   DISAPPOINTMENT

STORY

You'll recognize this cycle of disappointment as a backward-flowing cycle with fantasy, stories, and disappointment. It's backward moving because it focuses on the past to gather evidence about why something can't be done or why something didn't work, rather than moving forward to find out what's possible or make course corrections along the way.

Your quest in the cycle of fulfillment is to question any self-limiting story. And you can do this by asking, "What happened?" My son called me with a dilemma when he had a heavy metal band in the 90s. He was telling me how his band needed some public relations and how they had all decided on a plan and each one had made commitments to this plan. One of his band members made a commitment to call a list of twenty PR people. Here's what happened when they got back together to report on their progress. "No one wants to rep us," his band mates reported. My son asked, "Well, how many people did you call?" "Three." "Well, what did they say?" "They didn't call me back." "How many times did you call?" "Once ... I got disappointed so I didn't call back."

My friend Bill is a sales trainer. He told me that sales research shows you have to follow up seven to nine times before a sale is made. Most people don't follow up once. Few follow up twice. A training director in a large international organization told me he would get hundreds of proposals and pieces of information across his desk. He waited to see who would follow up because it told him something about the person and the company and their level of commitment.

In life we sometimes get disappointed, just like the member of my son's band. But if we let our disappointment stop us, we are buying into a cycle of disappointment that leads us to stop and find consolation in limiting stories. We believe that we're not accomplishing our goal because someone didn't call us back. And then we don't look at following up or what we could do or who else we could call. We step out of the field of possibilities.

The first step is to recognize your limiting stories when you tell them. See them for what they are—an interpretation of events that does not leave you with the power to be present with what's available in this moment. Once you "hear" yourself telling limiting stories, you can wake up and realize how you stop yourself right now, in this moment.

Find Your Inner Coach

You can trigger your inner guidance system—I call it your inner coach—by recognizing the stories you tell that stop you from going forward in the direction you say you want. Your inner coach can be annoying. It's the voice of commitment inside your head. Listen to your inner coach versus your excuse maker. Your inner coach will help you catch yourself in the act of making excuses. It's an extremely revelatory process. You stay awake and aware. Bring your attention to what you say to yourself and others. Catch yourself in the act of telling stories and making excuses. Interrupt yourself. Shift your attention to what you want. Remember, you set the goal. It's your vision of a life worth living. It's not a have-to; it's what you say you want. When you give up the limiting stories, you can explore whether it's truly what you want.

I'm not saying this is easy. Did you see the movie, *A League of Their Own*? Tom Hanks plays the coach of a women's baseball team and Geena Davis plays the star catcher. There's a scene where she says, "I'm leaving. This is too hard. I can't do it." Now what do you think the coach said? He says, "Hard? It's supposed to be hard. If it wasn't hard everyone would do it. It's the hard that makes it great." She kept playing. That's the job of a coach. A coach sees possibilities to move people out of the cycle of disappointment and incompletion, out of their limiting stories, even when their players don't see any possibilities. They have a commitment that is big enough to include the times when their players' commitment sags. The coach can't catch the ball for them but he can hold them accountable for their promises, explore possible solutions, and inspire them to stay on course. But there's one thing a coach can't do for you—they can't tell you what you want. Deciphering what you want—what you authentically want—is hard work and worth it.

Don't dismiss your vision and dreams as impossible or improbable; instead consider getting a coach, training, or additional education that might make the difference. If you can't imagine change, the tendency is to remain passive. You can start now to imagine change by recognizing your limiting stories and trade them in for what you truly want.

It's often easier to recognize someone else's limiting stories than your own. Resist the urge to enlighten them! If you want to develop your own inner coach and interrupt your self-limiting stories, ask yourself questions like:

"What could I do? What have I done so far?"
"What do I think is possible?"
"How can I get on track to accomplish my goal?"
"What are some ways to overcome this self-limiting story?"
"What help do I need? Who can I ask for help?"
"What am I learning?"
"What do I need to correct?"
"How do I make this a priority?"

Don't criticize or judge—that's not the job of your inner coach. Be interested and creative in your responses. The simple practice of noticing your limiting stories will change you. You may notice that you stop complaining and start taking action that fulfills you.

Practice: *Make a goal to catch yourself in the act of telling any self-limiting story. This is a perfect opportunity to develop your inner coach. If you notice that you are not keeping your promises, stop and ask yourself:*

What am I making more important than keeping my word and doing what I said I would do?

What am I making more important than being fulfilled?

Answer these questions without judgment. Once you notice your limiting stories, own up to them and laugh. This is the good news. Limiting stories are inside of your control. Bring to an end the need to tell the same old stories that have limited your actions up until now.

Once you understand the two cycles you can say, "Hmmm, it does have the ring of a limiting story." You can decide to stop telling the story and instead, allow your vision of being fulfilled today, to shape and organize your actions.

This is a mind-blowing experience because you start to wake up and see things as they are. Excuses drop away and change is possible. Notice for yourself what fills the space when excuses are absent. Krishnamurti in his discourses tells us to notice the behavior rather than try to change it. The change will come naturally as a result of seeing it as it is.

Chapter 5

Stop Arguing For Your Limitations

"You miss 100% of the shots you never take." Wayne Gretsky

We can't always control what happens to us or others, but we do have the power to think through our responses to what happens. We have the choice and the growing responsibility to shift away from our automatic reactions and be thoughtful and intentional in how we respond to requests, problems, circumstances, and interruptions.

Let's look at one of those automatic responses, "I don't have enough time." You might say that your job, family, or the conditions of your life are controlling your time, but that would put the problem outside of your control. If you don't have enough time, and you are in the cycle of fulfillment, you look at what's possible, instead of blaming conditions. What can you give up to achieve your goal? Or who can you get to help? Conduct a self-inquiry into what you're doing that fills up your time and leaves no room for anything new.

Think about that old saying "If you want something done, give it to a busy person." Busy people who are effective don't have a story about not having enough time. Time is what it is. They realize that sometimes they may have to sacrifice a non-essential priority in order to get a high priority finished. It's a shift in focus. When I'm concentrating on completing a project, I sacrifice chat time on the phone, email, or in person.

People understand and respect commitment, but you have to tell them. Don't expect them to know your deadlines or commitments; otherwise you'll just come across as impatient or imply there's something wrong with them for not knowing how busy you are. When peoople ask me, "Are you busy?" I say, "Yes, I'm up against a deadline." And the tone of the conversation is friendly, connected, and clear. We get to the point faster.

You may as well stop and tell the truth because they'll know when you are trying to split your attention between them and what you're doing on your computer. Look up, connect, be present, and tell the truth.

If you're operating in a cycle of disappointment, you'll wish you had the time, and you'll believe, incorrectly, that there's nothing you can do to have the space, resources, or people to get something done. This belief hides the fact that you can make a request for help and ask for coaching. You also might not consider the resources available to you, and most likely won't consider dropping some unimportant activities to make the time to have what you want and be fulfilled.

When you set a goal make sure it's what you want. What will the goal fulfill? Is it important to you? Think about it for a moment. What are some of the activities you now engage in that are non-essential and could be sacrificed in order to achieve this goal? Maybe for you it's reading catalogs or putting new tabs on your file folders so you can be more organized; or maybe it's talking on the phone, watching TV, playing video games, or surfing the net. Be aware of any regular activities that replace the kind of creativity or action you could take to fulfill what you say you want. Notice when you don't proactively look for what you could do to accomplish your goals, in contrast to looking for why it won't work.

The cycle of fulfillment includes choice, planning, and ownership. It's based on the behavioral imperative of accountability that says:

I can change, my organization can change, and the world can change, and not only can something be done, I can do it.

Instead of accountability the cycle of disappointment is based on a mental paradigm of conditionality—the belief that one is bound by conditions, circumstances, other people, and/or the past. This kind of thinking results in the idea that there's nothing you can do, and there's nothing anyone else can do either. So you may not make requests of yourself or others, or consider anything new or outside the boundaries of current conditions and excuses. Why would anyone think that? Because entertaining the possibility that someone can do it begs the question why not you?

Imagine using the fulfillment model so you can focus on shifting to the forward-moving cycle in the areas of your life where you want change. This could bring you fulfillment now because you'd be in action now. Have you ever noticed that as soon as you're in action you actually feel better? You don't have to wait until the end to be fulfilled. Fulfillment is in the action you take right now.

I'm not as interested in why we tell limiting, self-defeating stories as I am in bringing awareness to the behavior. I'm interested in shifting focus away from automatic reasons and reactions, to actually being present to notice what is happening now, unbound by past interpretations.

Let your commitment to what you want to achieve be unconditional. Listen. Ask questions. Revisit your vision. Let it inspire and organize your actions. You can do it. Explore possibilities that leave you and others in action. Don't bury your head in the sand—see things as they are. Meet obstacles with attention and discover something new, untried.

I continue to learn nuances in the art of recognizing limiting stories. Many years ago I taught coaching in a program I developed, called The Advanced Leadership Academy. In the beginning when participants wanted to change their goal I'd let them, thinking they saw something they didn't see when they initially set the goal. A most interesting thing happened. At the end of the program these same people said the reason they didn't accomplish the goal was that I let them off the hook. I could have argued with them and privately thought, *Wow, what a story!* But it had a ring of truth. It was really good feedback. And I didn't do it again. In fact, I let people know in the beginning that once they set the goal for the duration of the course, which lasted over a six-month period, I wouldn't let them change their goal.

How many times do we change our commitments, while the reasons why we wiggled out of our commitments go unnoticed as limiting stories? Do you ever notice that we don't simply change our commitment and just move on? There seems to be a limiting story to accompany the change. With that in mind I made the decision to hold participants' feet to the fire of their commitment. The result was that everyone considered very carefully the commitments they made. It was a good practice. Hold yourself and others accountable for promises made today, and you'll find fulfillment now rather than later. You'll use your creativity to find solutions … so much more fun than using your creativity to invent excuses.

It may be that from time to time Roger Bannister's commitment sagged. But imagine if he went to his team members and said, "Gee, do you really think we can do this?" What do you think they would say? "Nah, I think we should give up." Or "Why don't we just change the goal to something we know we can achieve? Let's see if we can just break the last record rather than try to break this impossible record." I don't think so! I heard Joseph Biden say that his mother told her children, "You can make mistakes, but you can never give up!" I agree.

Letting Go Of Your Excuses

Using this fulfillment model allows you to intervene in the limiting stories that prevent you from taking continuous action toward your goals. Once you hear your excuses as limiting stories, you can and will catch yourself in the act of making excuses. Then you can stop, sometimes mid-sentence, and own up to the fact that what you're saying limits your range of action.

In fact, if you stick to your story, it's an indication you are more committed to being right about why you can't do it, than you are committed to your goal. You're actually arguing for your limitations. This is an important awareness and fulfillment practice. When you find yourself arguing for your limitations, shine the light of inquiry into your words and the meaning behind them. Look into it. What's the source of your argument? What request or resource does the limitation conceal? What do you need? What's possible? What are you committed to? Just notice. Then take the action that will keep your focus on what you want to achieve, instead of shifting your focus to what you don't want.

Think for a moment. Who told you a limiting story recently about why something couldn't get done? Did it sound like an excuse? Often the way we handle listening to excuses is to try to talk someone out of them by saying things like, "Well, you're just not being positive. You could do it if you tried," or "Man, you need an attitude adjustment!" Maybe if you're in a position of power you even give them a little threat, "You better get it done!" Or perhaps bored silence is your response, wondering why you have to listen to this story over and over.

If talking them out of their story doesn't work, maybe you'll try giving them a little advice. Do you know how you listen to advice when you're certain that nothing will work? You might say things like, "Well, you just don't understand what's going on here." These responses don't do anything to get at what happened, or to shift someone from the cycle of disappointment into the cycle of fulfillment. Realize that it's always harder to recognize your own stories than someone else's stories. Why? Your stories sound like the truth to you! This is also true for the people who are telling you their stories. Their stories sound like the truth to them.

Once you begin to recognize your own limiting stories you'll also realize that the stories you continue to tell have a way of becoming self-fulfilling prophecies. You'll find what you seek! When you're stuck in a limiting story, talk to someone who is not bound by the same story as you and it can open up a world of possibilities.

What Cycle Are You In?

I often get asked what I do when people come to me for coaching on their limiting stories. First, I show them a diagram of the cycle of fulfillment contrasted with the cycle of disappointment, which sits on my desk. Then I ask, "Which cycle do you think you're operating in?"

Cycle Of Fulfillment

Where am I operating today?

Cycle Of Disappointment

Accountability

People know if they want me to coach them, I see them as accountable for what they are currently doing and what they are not doing. In fact, I often use the following question to provide a window into accountability: *What are you creating, promoting, or allowing in your life today?* The answer allows you to think about how you want to make up your life now, instead of waiting for some future, undefined time. There is no blame in accountability; not in the inquiry, not of yourself, others, or the conditions you find yourself in. I've had conversations with people suffering from illness who compound their struggle by blaming themselves for creating the illness. I encourage them to take blame out of the equation, so they can look through the eyes of accountability and discover what they can do today. Accountability brings you present so you can start where you are and look forward.

I use accountability as a discovery tool so I can learn and see what's revealed when I don't hide behind blame, excuses, and self-limiting stories. Stories can be a defense mechanism. You may find that your story is more desirable than facing reality. It may be easier for you to say you don't have the time than to face the reality of getting up earlier to accomplish what you say is important to your fulfillment.

Accountability provides a real opportunity to look at your responses to what is happening right now in your life. What do you want to do and what is possible if you stand accountable for what is showing up in your life today?

Accountability gives you a view of the impact and influence you have in your life right now. As you practice accountability, you can ask yourself if what you're doing is

58

what you want to promote, create, or allow in your life. These questions create an opening to look for possibilities, make a plan of action with time lines, and a strategy for follow-up and completion. If you have a hard time coming up with any ideas that result in action, it's probably an indication you don't want to do it, no matter what the opportunity.

The Desire To Change

If I were to ask you what you want, you would probably tell me you want a change of some kind. It could be a change in income, job, weight, health, happiness or something else that is important to you. Wanting change is the first step.

Here is the conundrum. You may say that you want change, yet you don't want to change your actions, or your behavior, or your thinking. I know! It is hard. You may want change but *you* don't want to change!

Understanding the cycle of fulfillment and the cycle of disappointment can be a real wakeup call for what it takes to make a commitment to change.

Someone asked me recently how I recognize commitment. Well, that's easy. Look at what is around you right now. Look at your daily practice. Whatever you find, that is what you're committed to today.

Practice: *Listen to yourself. Listen to what you say to yourself and to others. If you continue to notice any limiting stories add the following phrase "up until now" to what you say in either thought or words, then notice what happens to the limiting story.*

You'll find that whatever you say about how you have limited yourself up until now is a historical account. Even if you have an abundance of evidence to support your historical account, it's only true to this point in time. "Up until now" shifts your focus to what's possible in this present moment and opens a space to include what you want. "Up until now" creates a clearing for fulfillment. The moment to change your thinking is right now. Then your behavior and results change.

Chapter 6

Clearing The Blocks To Fulfillment

"The greatest block to progress isn't ignorance; it's the illusion of knowledge." Anon

Let's say you are recognizing the limiting statements you make. Imagine that those statements are like alarm clocks waking you up. Words create. If you want to create a future that is different from the past, start by changing your words to be in alignment with what you want. If this is a challenge for you, begin by noticing if you have a hard time making the following three simple statements:

"I don't know."
"I made a mistake."
"I need your help."

These can be, and often are, three difficult statements for people to make and can throw up blocks to progress in thoughts, words, and action. Why is it hard to acknowledge you don't know, or made a mistake, or need help? Is it image, ego, or the need to be perfect? What's hard or difficult for you to overcome is actually what builds strength, intelligence, and stamina. It's like running a hurdle race. You begin jumping over the low hurdles first. You start where you are. You get some training and coaching on how to get the lift you need to make it over the hurdle. It takes practice to recognize what stops you from making a request for help, or owning up to a mistake, or just saying you don't know when you don't.

The blocks to making these three statements are hurdles on the field of action and impact your communication, relationships, and overall fulfillment. You can clear these blocks anytime you want. It just takes practice.

Clearing Block #1: Pretending To Know

Practice saying "I don't know" or "How can I get the information?" or "What's the best place to start?" instead of pretending you know something you don't. These questions may sound obvious but pretending to know is rampant! Have you ever been in a situation where someone was talking and you had no idea what they were talking about, but you nodded your head as if you did and then the person said, "You know what I mean?" The tendency on our part is to say yes, even when we don't know what they mean. Now, maybe it's to be polite or maybe your mother told you not to ask too many questions or maybe you feel your image is at stake. Regardless of where it comes from, it makes "I don't know" a difficult statement to say. What can you do when somebody says, "You know what I mean?" Even if your first tendency is to say yes, shift to catching yourself in the act of agreeing when you don't and pause. Then you can say, "No, actually I don't know what you mean."

"I don't know" is the pause that refreshes and allows for discovery to take place. "I don't know" begins an inquiry that can lead to new information. "I don't know" has you give up the expectation that you should already know ... everything!

I've had people tell me they're so concerned with saying "I don't know" that they'll leave a meeting after their manager has given them information or instructions to do something, and they realize they don't know how to get started or what their manager's objective was. I'll ask them, "Why didn't you ask?" and they'll say, "I didn't want to sound stupid" or "When I ask, my manager just gets impatient."

Have you ever asked for something, and the person you requested it from took the time to do it, only it wasn't what you wanted? They didn't want to say, "I don't know what you want" and you didn't take the time to make sure they did. If you're operating from fulfillment, you make sure you are clear on what, when, who, how, and where. Sometimes just "Do you have any questions? Anything unclear?" will assist people to say they don't know or are unclear about what you're asking for.

The skill is to stay present while you're asking the questions and stay present while you're waiting for the response. Take a full minute and wait. Do you ever ask a question while you're shuffling papers or picking up the telephone? This kind of behavior signals that something else is more important than the person in front of you. In effect it's a dismissal. Show interest in their response to your question by waiting and engaging with them.

If someone says, "I don't know" to you, listen to it as a request for more information. They might not say those exact words. They might say, "I need some clarity," "I need direction," "I need training," or "I'm confused." If you listen to what's behind the questions or statements, you'll hear requests for assistance, guidance, and coaching; then clear action can be discussed and taken.

Listening is foundational to relationships that matter, whether at home or at work.

There's an old story about a man who goes to the East to find a master guru. He finally finds the one he is seeking and asks how he can improve his life. He is relentless in his questioning of the master. The master doesn't answer and simply suggests they have tea. As the master pours the tea, the gentleman imparts all of his accomplishments, concerns, and successes. The master just continues to pour the tea into the teacup until it starts to overflow. The self-absorbed aspirant blurts out, "What are you doing? The cup is overflowing!" The master stops and says, "Just as the teacup is full and has no more room, so are you filled with what you know, with no more room for anything new."

Learn to let go of concerns about what others may think of you, when you authentically acknowledge you don't know. Empty yourself of pre-conceived answers when you ask a question, so you can listen and be present for the response. Release impatience when you respond to questions, and recognize them as necessary to achieve the best outcome.

Clearing Block #2: Pretending To Never Make A Mistake

An idea gaining momentum in organizations today is the importance of creating continuous learning environments. In one organization I worked with we called it a correctible process. In order to have a continuous learning environment or a correctible environment, there has to be a focus on accountability. Even though the idea is to get it right the first time, when mistakes happen, smart leaders admit it and fix the problem.

There is a high commitment to telling the truth about mistakes in a correctible environment. What is your tolerance for mistakes? The dictionary defines tolerance as a fair and objective attitude. That means mistakes are listened to in a fair and objective manner. Mistakes in a continuous learning environment are seen as opportunities for improvement. I think it's an unrealistic expectation to think mistakes are never going to happen and that notion can create a culture of fear. When people operate in fear they don't take risks and they cover up their mistakes. They try to have a perfect environment instead of a productive environment.

Problems and mistakes happen when you set big goals. It's essential for your success to acknowledge when mistakes happen. You might not say the exact words, "I made a mistake." You might say, "I've got a problem to solve." And when mistakes happen you want them to be identified and corrected quickly. If you have a coaching environment, it's easier to own up to a mistake and resolve it. If you don't know how to correct it, you ask for coaching. Mistakes are problems to be solved and lessons to be learned. When mistakes are declared and acknowledged you learn the lesson. You don't gloss over it, you find out what happened. You want to ensure that even when you lose the customer, the employee, the sale, or the game, you don't lose the lesson. Learning the lesson prevents mistakes from happening again.

As soon as a mistake is acknowledged you start to solve the problem rather than point the finger. I was in a meeting and we were going over the same ground on a systems integration issue until an executive acknowledged he'd made the decision, and it wasn't working. The atmosphere in the room shifted immediately. The shift from excuses and reasons to accountability and solutions cleared the air. Everyone took a breath and began to focus on defeating the problem instead of blaming each other. It was refreshing and powerful to hear him take responsibility for the problem. He declared the breakdown and acknowledged what happened so we could define the issue, determine what was possible, and move into action to solve the problem.

Accountability for mistakes is the foundation of breakthrough thinking. You can see further when you take accountability for the problem. Why? You're not pretending that something is working when it's not. You're also not giving up by acting like you've done everything you can do. You may have done everything you "know" how to do. Accountability moves you to stand at the boundary of the known and the unknown. Breakthroughs happen in the unknown. Accountability starts the process of inquiry so mistakes can be corrected. The statement "I made a mistake" turns into a powerful declaration that stops the action so a resolution, a new direction, a different strategy, can be implemented.

Clearing Block #3: Pretending To Never Need Help

Making the request "I need your help" can often be seen as a high hurdle to jump. People tell me they don't want to be seen as weak and they believe that asking for help is an admission of weakness. This belief must be challenged and changed. Asking for help can actually build relationships, forge a team, and develop strength and conviction. The result is that you can take on goals bigger than you can accomplish alone.

It seems to me that organizations are set up for people to ask for and receive help. In fact, one of the common reasons people give when they don't accomplish their goals is that they couldn't get any help. But when you ask those same people whether they made a request for help they'll often say no, and if offered help, they refused. You don't have to wait until it's an emergency to ask for help. Set it up in the beginning as part of your strategy to get things done or as soon as you realize you're at risk.

Often the same person who won't ask for help doesn't delegate either. Have you heard the story that it takes too much time to train someone else, or it's just easier to do it yourself? I find that it's actually a waste of time to continue doing what someone else can do. Delegating frees you up to do what's important.

I had a co-worker who would see every offer of help as an attack on her effectiveness. When she would finally delegate some work, she wouldn't give the person all the information, as if the sharing of information would decrease her power. It was a self-fulfilling prophecy. She wanted to take on more responsibility but was refused a promotion because of this trait. The quality of her work actually suffered as a result of having to do everything herself. No amount of coaching worked because she couldn't disengage from the idea that asking for help was a sign of weakness and consider that asking for help could be a sign of intelligence.

An effective person knows that the bigger the project the more you have to delegate. It's important to delegate with wisdom. My son is a producer and account director in the home entertainment industry. He told me he doesn't delegate, he "regulates." I asked him what that meant. He told me most managers "dump" work that they don't want to do with little instruction on how to do it, or even give a context for why it needs to be done. He gives instruction and a context and one more thing. He follows up on a continual basis so the person knows what to produce and when to produce it. He shows that he's interested in them and committed to the result. So what happens? He gets more projects, people in the company want to work for him (they know they can ask him for help), and his clients love him!

I've also worked with a person who delegated "up" and was always asking for help unnecessarily. He just wanted to get what he didn't like to do off his plate even though the work was clearly his responsibility. He liked directing others, had no problem delegating ... everything! I needed him to actually do some work. Asking for help or pleading ignorance was an excuse.

Spending your energy on strategies to get out of work and your commitments, is a strong indication that you don't want to be where you are. Being honest with yourself will move you to think about a change to what makes you happy.

Practice: *Make these statements—"I don't know," "I made a mistake," or "I need your help"— when that is the authentic response or request.*

Use this practice to create opportunities for improving performance by asking questions, telling the truth and taking responsibility for your action or inaction. Creating a culture of fulfillment in your relationships and on the job makes it easier to jump over any hurdles to making these three statements authentically.

It's liberating when you stop pretending. What can emerge is a genuine conversation about what's possible.

Chapter 7

Suspending Reaction

"A moment of patience instead of anger prevents a thousand days of sorrow." Rumi

As you clear any remaining limiting stories or any hurdles to your fulfillment, you begin to realize mistakes, failures, and obstacles are part of the process of getting things done. They are actually part of fulfillment. Mistakes are an important process of life. Mistakes happen! They trigger your resourcefulness. They actually cause you to wake up and see things as they are.

Notice what happens when you don't get what you want or something doesn't go your way. The action in your reaction is determined by habit, training, and what you believe is possible. Reactions that are beneficial are often described later as "thinking on your feet, training kicked in, and cool under fire." How you react to what is showing up in your daily life of work, presentations, traffic, and family is as important as how you react in an emergency. In any situation trading a harmful reaction for being fully present and paying attention will give you insight and awareness around what is happening. Harmful reactions (anger, frustration, bitterness, embarrassment, self-judgment or blame) limit your range of thoughts, words, and actions.

I recognized early on in life that it wasn't that I made mistakes or failed; it was how I reacted and what I did in response that made a difference. The response that made the biggest difference was not giving up! I took geometry in high school and received a D. It was awful. I just didn't get it. I could have blamed the teacher or my ability to learn abstract ideas but I didn't. Instead I took the class again and received an A. I learned an invaluable lesson: whatever I'm committed to I can learn. This is as true with a diet, exercise, or a new career, or listening to "difficult" people as it is with geometry. I carry this awareness with me into all new ventures.

When you operate from fulfillment you put mistakes into context. If you never make any mistakes, you're probably not taking any risks. What is a risk worth taking? If you want to get on in life and do what you dream, you'll take on what you don't already know how to do and realize you'll make mistakes along the way.

However, fear of making mistakes won't stop you.

Have you ever taken a course in a foreign language? Did you expect that you would already know how to speak the language in advance of the first class? No, of course not. And you don't have an expectation that you're going to speak perfectly after the first class. You keep on practicing and then one day you're speaking the language.

However in other areas of life you may suffer from the disease of perfection. Progress keeps you moving forward. An unrealistic view of perfection can stop you. How do you get moving in the direction you want to go and make progress each day? How do you even start the thought process so you're free to think and act in new ways?

I suggest you create a mistake-free zone. It's a powerful

mental construct and is the antidote to the disease of perfection. It's the opportunity to imagine your success. Putting mistakes in this context is important. I'll give it some extra attention here because for me it's the difference between growth and fulfillment and excuses and stagnation.

A mistake-free zone is a thinking zone, a non-defensive reaction to what happens. It's the opportunity to try on new ideas and take on new goals in the absence of excessive concern. It allows you to give up guarding against the real or imagined threat of criticism, injury to your ego, or exposure of your shortcomings. In a nutshell, it's the freedom to think and act, and allows you to suspend reactions that may have stopped you up until now from engaging fully in your dreams and goals.

Maybe it's because I grew up in Hollywood that I think of a mistake-free zone as missed takes. I can actually see the director saying, "Okay, quiet on the set, take 1." And what follows? Take 2, take 3, and maybe take 87! You don't give up and you get the "take." A mistake-free zone happens when you suspend reaction to what is occurring and resolve the issue. You see things as they are and you take new action that will move you forward to achieve your intended result. TAKE 2!

Resistance to what happened causes reaction. Resistance.Have you ever heard the saying, "What you resist persists?" Instead of resisting or feeling guilty, ask yourself "What can I do that makes a difference and leaves me and others both in action and fulfilled?"

First you have to acknowledge you made a mistake.

Feedback On Mistakes

Now think about how difficult it is to talk to someone who hears any reflection on mistakes or what they did or didn't do as criticism. Some people get offended when you give them feedback even when they asked you for it. If you're giving feedback you don't want to be excessively critical about what happened. Just give the facts. When you listen to feedback about a mistake, you don't have to get offended or beat yourself up. Where's the balance? And where's the point of power? It's in the way you speak and listen. That's the good news. You don't have to wait for someone else to operate non-defensively for you to operate non-defensively and to be fulfilled. You are not at the mercy of how someone speaks or listens to you. That's a powerful wakeup call. Your behavior is not predicated on how someone else acts. You can create a non-defensive environment that fosters creativity, truth-telling, generous listening, and a culture of fulfillment by suspending your reaction. Reactive, self-protective minds foster attack and defend as a strategy to resolve problems and listen to feedback. What can you do instead?

Listen to feedback as information.

Give feedback with an intention to make someone great. I have a friend who is a ballerina. She took dance classes to join a national ballet troupe and if she didn't get very direct, critical feedback from the instructor, she knew she wasn't going to make the cut. "Nice job" doesn't help a dancer (or you) improve. When someone is committed to your success, they give you specific information that moves you forward in your life, career, and relationships. The key was how she listened to the feedback. She listened with the thought in mind that the teacher was there to improve her performance as a ballerina.

If you have an authentic relationship with someone, you can talk about anything. When you're free to speak and listen, you're operating in a mistake-free zone. It comes from a generosity of spirit instead of a need to be right.

It takes practice to hear feedback as information, especially criticism, and not react. I hear criticism as feedback. It's not fun yet I look for the truth in what's being said. If it's there, I find it. If it's not, I let it go. I have a practical approach to discerning the truth in feedback when it's not obvious to me. Instead of just dismissing it, I ask clarifying questions like: "What specifically did you notice?" or "What would have been more effective?" or "What were you looking for that was missing?" I ask these questions against a background of genuine interest. I'm not infallible. Feedback allows me to learn and grow both in skills and as a human being. I also will ask someone who knows me well and is not invested in the situation to give me an assessment or coach me.

If you are willing to create a mental mistake-free zone, you're empowered to see life as it is and listen to feedback without the veil of your pre-determined opinions—and you start to let go of attachment to be seen as right in every situation.

Have you ever cared for certain individuals—family, co-workers, or friends—and that prevented you from seeing them as they really are? Perhaps you glossed over their mistakes and made excuses for behavior you wouldn't excuse in others. I've seen this happen time after time in organizations when performance reviews are conducted. Notice how "liking" someone can influence your evaluation. This works in a similar fashion with people you don't like or you think judge you or your work. You may be excessively critical or judgmental. Don't let your "like/dislike" meter get in the way of listening to or giving feedback. Some of the best and most honest feedback can come from someone who isn't under your influence or in your network of support.

That's why someone who is "neutral" and who is looking at results can review a performance appraisal for objectivity. Could you be impartial and practice a mistake-free zone in your work relationships so you are free to speak and give relevant feedback?

When you practice a mistake-free zone, you're ready to listen with the purpose of being present and attentive to what someone else has to say. Telling the truth or asking a well-placed question brings forward a response. Someone may not agree with you, or you may not agree with him or her. Can your relationship withstand a conflict or a difference of strategy or opinion? I believe that until you have a collision of ideas, you don't know whether you have a true relationship that will stand the test of honesty.

Have you ever asked someone to tell you the truth? "Just tell me the truth," you say. When you make that request you're invoking a mistake-free zone. You're saying to the other person that you're listening with interest and giving them permission to speak freely. What happens if they put the issue on the table and you get upset or defensive? You ask them to tell you the truth and they do. Notice how you respond. If you explode, get miffed, be dismissive or politely gloss over the information, give the silent treatment, consider the source as stupid, unconscious, not spiritual, not focused on results, not experienced or too emotional, then you're giving up an opportunity to learn something that could be of value. You're also giving up an opportunity to build trust in a relationship.

Whatever is your "favorite" reaction strategy, they boil down to: fight, flight, or be polite! What goes along with asking for the truth is the ability to suspend your reaction long enough to listen. Listen and say thank you for the courage it takes to give authentic feedback.

To suspend reaction takes practice!

How you listen to each person is different. Listening to some people may be easy for you. You sit back, you don't react, you collaborate, you're engaged, you coach, you empathize, the problem gets solved, an action plan gets implemented, and the relationship gets stronger. With other people it may be more difficult for you to listen. You may find yourself cutting them off, interrupting them, or giving them the answer just to get them out of your space. You don't have to practice with the people with whom you're already effective. Your practice is suspending reaction with people who are difficult for you. People differ in style, desire, and attitude. You learn to speak with them, to engage them and encourage them, regardless of their style, words, or approach if you want to be effective with a wide range of people. It takes practice.

I was coaching a business associate. (Name changed to protect the innocent.) *Joan* had a co-worker who didn't hand in some important paperwork on time. When she realized the project deadline was at risk, she just got angrier with her co-worker. This wasn't the first time these two folks clashed. When she saw that her reaction to what happened replaced any other possibilities, she started to reconsider her own behavior. What she realized is she did a slow boil, didn't say anything to her co-worker or confront her missing the commitment, didn't negotiate an alternative or get a new commitment. Now, she did give her co-worker a number of angry reminders, which were all ignored. Joan's usual response would be to just do it herself and complain. But in this instance that wasn't possible.

What do you do when you think you've tried everything? When you suspend judgment you start thinking outside of what you already know. Your commitment is to come up with a possibility that will solve the problem.

Joan got creative and asked a vendor working on the project to get the paperwork and follow up. It was clearly in the vendor's interest to make sure all the paperwork was in. If they ran into a problem, they could bump it up the chain of command or ask a simple question of the errant co-worker: "What's in the way of you getting this done?" Once that question was actually asked and answered, Joan, her co-worker, and the vendor discovered what needed to be done. Problem solved. The enduring realization for Joan was recognizing that once she "judged" a person, it was difficult for her to back off, make a new request, and see that person differently.

Listening To Different Styles Of Communication

People do have different styles. Some people may be more dominating, more aggressive. Some may be analytical or enthusiastic. Some may be more controlling or more supportive, outgoing, or reflective. If you can only listen to one style, it's hard to be effective. If you're in reaction to some styles, you'll find yourself consistently disappointed.

How do you suspend reaction? The key is to listen non-defensively to people, regardless of how they bring an issue to you or how they communicate. This is easier said than done.

If I'm in reaction, I have to remind myself to slow down and listen. Breathe! My job is to listen. If at first others seem hesitant, that may be just part of their style. Your style may be decisive. Their style might be careful, deliberate, and analytical. They may not want to come up with possibilities or make decisions on the spot. So what do you do? Invoke a mindful, mistake-free zone and suspend reaction. When you stop reacting, you engage your ability to think clearly and respond effectively. You become more powerful in all your interactions.

For you to be effective, learn to work with styles that are different from yours. Some people may be more formal. People may want more structure than you like to give them, or less structure than you'd like. They may want to know your reasoning. They may ask a lot of questions. They may be very direct.

I've been teaching communication styles for many years. One of the processes has the participants ask each other how to work with their particular style more effectively— especially those that are most different from theirs. The answers are varied depending on the style, but there is one response that is consistent regardless of style, and that is a key factor in being successful. Do you know what it is? Every single group said the way you could work with them more effectively is to listen. Just listen.

Now, the analytical style usually says, "Listen to me longer than you're comfortable with. I take cognitive breaks. You have to listen through the silence." The more promoting style says, "Listen to me with all my energy. Include my enthusiasm. Don't cut me off. Listen to me thoroughly." The supporting style says, "Ask me how I feel and listen to my feelings. Respect my emotions." The more controlling, driving style says, "Listen to the facts of the matter. Listen unemotionally and objectively."

Your ability to work with anyone is correlated with your ability to listen and to see things as they are. Keep your focus on resolution. Not everyone is like you. When you realize people have different styles it makes your job of working or living with someone easier. You think about how you can speak and listen in a way that moves a conversation forward. Your commitment to listening needs to be bigger than your initial reaction, so you can do what it takes to not attack, defend, acquiesce, or leave. If you notice that you're reacting, you might say to someone, "Give me a minute." And actually take that moment to clear some space in your mind. Remember "Take 2" and then focus on the person. Be present. Why? What's required to listen isn't to know the answer in advance but to be present to find out.

The Choice To Listen

When suspending reaction so you can listen transcends from an idea to a practice, it doesn't take long to acknowledge when you're in reaction. It's hard to pretend. You know when you'd rather be right than resolve the situation.

How do you consistently suspend reaction? In order to suspend reaction you have to first notice you're reacting and that you're reacting in a way that stops the flow of information or the flow of love. If people think they are going to cause a major reaction in you, they are less likely to bring information freely, raise questions, make requests, tell the truth, or ask for help.

Examine your intention in situations where you notice you react with an attack or defend strategy. If your co-workers or members of your family described your habitual mode when bringing you problems, what might they say about you? Will they say you listen? Or will they say you react? Or will they say it's hit-and-miss depending on your mood?

One of the most powerful personal realizations I've had, and continue to have, is that my behavior is not based on anyone else's behavior. Meaning that because someone else is angry doesn't mean that I need to get angry. Because someone else attacks, doesn't mean I have to attack. Because someone else defends, doesn't mean I have to get defensive. As soon as you recognize it's your choice you can shift very effectively.

If I notice for example that I'm getting impatient, I take a slow breath and tell myself to just listen. If I notice I'm angry, I stop and take a break. I take some time to think. If I can, I go for a run. I also take the freedom, in the moment, not to respond. No one can push you for a response. And you know what? It seems I have less to clean up after the fact if I don't respond out of reaction.

The practice is to wake up and notice. Then act out of conscious intention rather than reaction.

Practice: *Suspend reaction. Take one breath before you speak ... inhale and exhale. This only takes 3 to 7 seconds. Then pause and get more interested in what someone has to say. You can ask questions and find out what happened.*

If you notice you're getting righteous, or you're attached to an idea, or exhibiting an attitude of "my way or the highway," you can say, "Wait a moment. I'm doing all the talking. This is just one idea. Tell me what you think." And then listen.

If you are awake to your own reactions and you're interested in building your relationships, you can stop the game, call a timeout, clear your head, take a walk, breathe or ask a question.

Recognize you don't make people strong by calling them weak. And you don't make them capable by seeing them as ineffective. You don't make them winners by calling them losers, in your thoughts or in your words. See mistakes as opportunities to tell the truth with love and correct the problem. Separate the people and their styles from the problem at hand. Ask yourself not what's wrong with yourself or another, but how you can be more effective.

Suspending reaction is an important fulfillment practice and in relationships is essential for being effective at work and at home.

Chapter 8

Creating A Mistake-Free Zone

"If I ran a school, I'd give the average grades to the ones who gave me all the right answers, for being good parrots. I'd give the top grades to those who made a lot of mistakes and told me about them, and then told me what they learned from them." R. Buckminster Fuller

Let's look at establishing a culture of fulfillment at work. Your job is a great place to practice suspending reaction and creating a mistake-free zone. You work every day primarily with the same group of people so why not set up a way to play the game of work so you're fulfilled?

Brainstorming

Have you ever been in a brainstorming meeting where everyone is instructed to come up with any possibility, however outrageous, with the intention of discovering an idea "outside the box?" Outside the box means outside what you already know or have already decided. It's outside your current thought and what you've been conditioned to believe by your family, business, successes, and failures. It's challenging to do, which is why so many brainstorming sessions fail. Sometimes they fail because there's a mistaken idea that just talking about something is the same as getting it done. But more often they fail because ideas are shot down and thinking creatively stops.

A mistake-free zone is fundamental to true brainstorming, whether it's being mindful of your own internal process with one other person, or with a group of people.

Several years ago I began to declare training programs and meetings at work as mistake-free zones. In the beginning, I asked the participants to tell me what a mistake-free zone would provide for them. They said it would create an environment where the truth could be told. In fact, in meetings I've had people say, "Okay, I'm going to find out whether this really is a mistake-free zone." And then they test it by saying what's on their mind and seeing whether there are any repercussions. They want to find out whether people will actually listen to what they have to say non-judgmentally. In a mistake-free zone people tell me they can be themselves. They can be creative and have direct communication with each other instead of complaining. They can solve problems and talk about anything. And most importantly they can listen and be engaged in the process. In a brainstorming session they can come up with ideas no matter how outrageous; they're encouraged to be outrageous and go where no one has gone before.

So how will you know you're thinking and operating in the unknown? You'll notice an absence of automatic responses. You'll notice untested ideas. You'll notice a willingness to postulate (something that may be obvious and correct but can't be proven) so you can look into what's possible given that postulation. You'll consciously turn reason on its head. You'll have a tolerance for ambiguity. This is how you get people to think in the unknown and come up with new, ground-breaking ideas "outside the box."

Triangular Communication

I've also used the idea of a mistake-free zone to coach people to end "triangular communication." Triangular communication is a classic example of a defensive, reactive environment. It's when you don't talk to the person you're having the problem with; instead you talk to somebody else who can't make a difference. Think about the times you are the "someone else," the third person in triangular communication. Have you ever wondered or maybe even said, "Well, sounds like you need to talk to Joe. Why don't you just talk to him?" And what does the other person say? "Ah, he wouldn't listen." And they walk away to talk to the next person who will be a receptacle for their complaints.

**Complaining keeps you in a cycle of disappointment
where you operate as if change is not possible.**

Continual complaining is an indication of an attitude of resignation. Resignation keeps you stuck where you are. Resignation indicates that you believe there is nothing you can do. When you're fulfilled you don't complain. Instead, you turn your complaints into a request or a promise to get what you want done.

Acceptance instead of resignation is at the core of making a request or a promise. Acceptance allows you to see things as they are and determine what action is possible. You could just talk to the "Joe" in your life. Why doesn't someone just talk to Joe? They're probably afraid of the reaction they'll get. What they don't see is their own resistance and resignation. If they could listen in a "mistake-free zone," trust their resourcefulness to respond, and not have to know in advance what the outcome is going to be, they could actually have the conversation even when it's uncomfortable.

In a culture that fosters fulfillment you can have the "uncomfortable" conversations. A mistake-free zone becomes a process to make course corrections. It actually allows for people to address problems quickly instead of complaining about them. You can put an issue on the table so it can be addressed and resolved. A mistake-free zone allows for accountability—you can own up or coach someone else to own up without fear.

I find that often participants will carry over the notion of a mistake-free zone from their work meetings to their homes. What they discovered in declaring their meetings mistake-free zones is a freedom to speak and listen, and a freedom to see things as they are. They are willing to own up to issues, listen to others, and self-correct quickly. If you can own up to a problem and your family or co-workers can own up to problems, you can solve them faster because no one suffers from cover-up mentality. Cover-up mentality is increased when there is concern for what people are going to think, when there is fear of appearing stupid, ineffective, or ridiculous. This is usually an unwarranted fear. Saying "I've got a problem" is the first step to solving it.

Meetings

Have you ever been in a meeting where no one says anything but as soon as they're out the door they are all talking about the issues they're not bringing up in the meeting? These are "hallway conversations" and they create hurdles to an honest flow of communication. Imagine you could have those conversations in the meeting. A mistake-free zone allows you to address the issues you face every day on the job. If you can already come up with a solution, do it. If not, tell the truth. You don't have to pretend to have a solution when you don't.

I have a friend who's a nuclear physicist. He told me an interesting story that I think is relevant to the idea of putting mistakes into a context that gives you the freedom to act. When he first started working on artificial intelligence at MIT, he wanted to design a computer program that could learn from every transaction. He did this by designing a simple game. Do you know what he discovered? No matter how much he changed the program design, he found "intelligence" grew and "learning" happened only from mistakes, not from successes. Success could be replicated but progress was furthered by mistakes.

The computer is different in this story from human beings. A program takes the information from the mistake and integrates it and improves. Human beings tend to beat themselves up or feel bad or guilty about making the mistake. Or sometimes they'll try and cover it up so no one else knows. This is an error in thinking. I believe that who we are is big enough to include what we don't know. It's the foundation of discovery. It's important to find out what doesn't work and integrate the information a mistake provides as quickly as possible. Imagine sharing with other people the nature of the mistake and how it was corrected so no one else has to make that mistake. The computer program doesn't hide the mistake or suffer about it. Human beings don't have to hide the mistake or suffer from endless worry about being exposed. We can let cover-up mentality go along with suffering about mistakes.

If the greatest opportunities for learning happen when we make mistakes, then putting mistakes into perspective allows us to have setbacks and emerge stronger and smarter without stopping us from achieving our goals and living a fulfilled life.

Coaching In A Mistake-Free Zone

A wise person and an effective coach know when to intervene and when to wait. It's important if you have that role to let people know they can get coaching when mistakes happen. It's also important for the people you love. Mistakes are results. Mistakes give you information. The first question to ask is "What happened?" Then you can get the information you need to respond effectively.

People learn best in a non-defensive environment where the focus is on the problem, not on who they are or aren't as the case may be. An effective coach helps put the spotlight on the problem to be solved, and separates the person from the problem. Then they can focus on what behavior needs to change or what part of the process needs to change in order to produce the intended results.

Ask yourself who you are when you are talking to someone who made a mistake. Are you present, interested, compassionate? Who are you for that other person? What's your intention? Sometimes all you have to do is listen completely and be engaged in the conversation and the solution is revealed.

I was talking to my daughter recently about one of my business relationships. I was upset! I sent an email that was misinterpreted. My daughter is a coach for me. She's an experienced executive, non-judgmental, she's funny, and she listens. I knew I was judging the email recipient as a butthead and said something like, "I wish I could just smack him." She looked at me and said, "Sounds like he could use a hug." We both started laughing but it changed my thinking immediately. She knows that I stand for accountability not blame. Instead of blaming the other person for making my life hard, I took accountability for sending the email. I chose the words in the email and I could just as easily have given him a call to clear things up. So, I did. He was appreciative. Instead of holding on to being right, I cleared things up and our relationship improved. In fact my relationship improved with his whole department. Instead of making someone else wrong, I held myself accountable, and separated the problem from the person. Then I could solve the problem not from annoyance, but from connection and from the point of view that if we're going to win, we have to work together.

Accountability is the foundation of a mistake free-zone and gives you a window to see things as they are. No blame, just ownership. Accountability shifts the focus from what's wrong to what happened. This creates a doorway to discovering solutions and building relationships that produce lasting results. Mistakes allow you to discover what's missing.

Practice: *Create a mistake-free zone in your meetings and conversations to support listening and thinking outside the box. You can declare your meetings a mistake-free zone at the beginning of each meeting or in the middle of a contentious conversation so everyone can be heard.*

Mistakes happen. Growth is often a series of mistakes and corrections. Watch toddlers learning to walk. Time after time they fall down, and they keep getting up until they walk. Just like toddlers, when you fall down, get up one more time; and when others fall down remind them to never give up.

Chapter 9

Letting Go Without Giving Up

"Don't let what you cannot do interfere with what you can do."
John Wooden

Have you ever watched people dig in their heels when they're talking? When you see it happen you can feel the tension build. If you pull back a little from the situation, you can readily observe a few things. One is the absence of listening or any true exchange of ideas. You might notice someone who is demanding or intent on forcing an outcome. This is often exacerbated when the "someone" is in a position of authority. You may notice other people give up and walk away, resigned to the fact that they can't be honest or influence the outcome. Both attitudes—force and giving up—are the results of attachment to an outcome.

Attachment can happen in any conversation where there's a right way (mine) and a wrong way (yours). People will defend what they're attached to and they'll have a hard time being open to consider anything else. Instead of fulfillment, aggravation is the result of this type of communication.

When you are suffering from attachment there seems to be very little or no interest in a back-and-forth dialogue about what's needed, what happened, what could work, or what a shared vision of the future might look like. Attachment can rear its ugly head regardless of the topic of conversation when your need to be right is bigger than your openness to listen and engage in what's possible.

When I've asked people why they get attached to an outcome, they'll tell me that if they weren't attached nothing would get done! One person said that his communication was demanding so others would get the importance of his requests. I asked him whether that worked. Did he notice that people got things done for him faster? He admitted that it didn't always work and sometimes actually had the opposite effect. I asked him to consider making his requests without attachment.

A request with attachment is an aggressive demand where the only response allowed is yes, a forced choice.
A request without attachment allows a true response, a yes or no.

As he took on this practice he noticed his relationships at work improve because he could have an honest dialogue about what could be done and by when it would be completed. He also noticed that his stress level reduced almost immediately. He stopped having to get up a head of steam to make requests and get things done. He began to build a culture of fulfillment versus a culture of fear and complaints. He let go of his attachment because he noticed that it added stress to his communication and to getting things done ... and it was unnecessary.

In previous chapters you've seen two ways to create an opening to consider something new; first, engage a mindful mistake-free zone, and second, consciously suspend harmful reactions. The third way is to give up your attachment to an outcome without giving up your commitment to the outcome. There is a difference. What is the difference between attachment and commitment?

Commitment

Commitment is about performance and willingness. Commitment says you have a clear goal. You know why you're doing it and you'll do what it takes to achieve it. Even if it means you're learning a new skill. You seek feedback so you can make corrections along the way. Commitment indicates a level of participation that is dedicated to producing the result, regardless of obstacles or prevailing conditions. You're not waiting for the outcome to experience fulfillment; you're fulfilled in the actions you take along the way.

Attachment

Attachment says something different. When you get attached to an outcome, it's often because a little fear has crept in telling you that you're not going to achieve what you set out to do without forcing your strategy. Your focus shifts from performing to concern. And depending on your style, your communication can come across as demanding or pleading.

Now think about how you come across when you're communicating with attachment. Do you put pressure on yourself and others? Is it a "my way or the highway" attitude? Or do you ever just give up thinking that whatever you're doing won't work?

Attachment comes from a fear of loss ... a loss of relationship, image, or security. Have you read the list of things that people say cause them the most fear? Do you know what is often listed as number one? Fear of speaking in front of a group! That's an easy attachment to recognize. What will people think of you if you make a mistake in a presentation or in a meeting?

That attachment could prevent you from ever speaking up or making a presentation.

Another easy attachment to recognize is an overpowering need to be right. This one is often easier to recognize in someone else! They have to have the last word and want it to be done their way. They're the "not open for discussion" people.

Why do you get attached in the first place? You may think your job is at stake if you spoke up, or your relationship might be at stake if you told the truth, or your image could be at stake if you made a mistake. What's really at stake if you miss the outcome? I'm reminded of Mark Twain's statement that most of the things we worry about never come to pass. If what you worry about comes to pass attachment doesn't help. It actually hinders the process of determining what's possible and working out a solution. That's why third parties are often helpful to finding possibilities that others who are entrenched in a situation can't identify.

The energy of attachment comes across as force and the energy of commitment as inspiration. Attachment is an over-identification with an outcome. Think about a time when you were attached to an outcome. How did your attachment impact the performance you gave? Sport psychologists tell us when people get attached to a goal it impacts their performance in a negative way. Why? Attachment takes your focus off what you are doing now and puts your focus on the future with a concern about the outcome. You may start thinking, *How am I going to look? What's going to happen if I lose? What are people going to think of me?*

If you start thinking about what you're going to do if you lose, your attention wanders from being present to play, speak, and act now. When you notice any of these kinds of concerns, it's time to create some space in your thinking so you can consider a different way to be with your concerns.

Just noticing that you're attached helps relieve it. Take a breath and focus on what you want to create. Breathe in and out slowly. Meditate, do yoga, go for a run, go to the gym, take a walk around your office building, just stand up and start shaking it off! Increase your participation. There were times I noticed my attachment at work and I stood on my head in my office. It's amazing how different the world looks when you get upside down! Attachment starts to shrink when you don't feed it with frustration, anger, bitterness, resistance, inevitability, or unbending demands.

You may notice that when you're in action stress and concern diminish. You'll notice that you're in a forward motion to achieve your intended outcome. Low attachment and high participation include creating the space and time to think about how to overcome obstacles along the way. This is commitment. This is preparation. You're in the game playing full out when you operate from commitment. So instead of attachment that fills up your space with "worries" that don't resolve, or fills up your time with pressure about the future, consider letting go of any attachment. Let your commitment guide your focus, determination, and presence to live life fully.

How do you notice whether you're operating from attachment? The primary strategies you might play are using force (do it or else!), complaining (why doesn't anyone do this right?), or giving up (who cares?).

You can imagine what these attachment strategies do to the people you work with, and to achieving your intended results.

I worked with an executive recently who began to consider that his commitment was infused with attachment to the goal. He had attachment and commitment entangled together. This executive noticed his attachment was continually revealed in his conversations with co-workers. Instead of exploring possibilities or ideas with his colleagues, he started to strongly convince; instead of making requests of people for assistance, he would demand; and instead of listening, he would interrupt in order to enlighten people to the real and only solution. The result was that people wanted to do less and less for him. He especially noticed this when he was in the selling process. When he got attached to someone buying from him, he was more concerned with his own needs for the sale than for fulfilling the needs of the customer.

Attachment is intriguing because it can often masquerade as commitment. But attachment has an edge and puts blinders on you so you can't see anything outside of what you already believe is true, right, and effective, even when it's not working. It's the old definition of insanity ... doing the same things over and over expecting a different result. That's a clear demonstration of attachment!

If you are committed to the result and to finding solutions or ways of being that will keep you on track, why be attached to only one way to achieve the outcome? And if the solution you come up with is the right or best solution, why be attached to it? In conversations or discussion let the merit of the idea, solution, or goal determine the choice. When you get attached to an outcome, you will try to force it one way or another. And the "my way or the highway" attitude creates a defensive environment. People will decide in advance that there's no point in talking to you because you have already made a decision and there's no opening for anything new.

What do you notice physically when you're attached? Do you feel it as a tightening in your stomach? Do you feel it as a pressure in your head? Some people report they feel it as a pressure across their shoulders, like they're walking around with a burden. I notice when I get attached what goes along with it is impatience and a change in my tone of voice. My communication can become demanding and harsh, impacting relationships, team building, and results. There are different clues to recognizing your attachment so you can catch yourself in the act and let it go.

I worked with someone who listened to feedback as if she was being attacked. Her attachment showed up as "don't tell me what to do" and limited her ability to listen effectively until she could replace it with a different strategy.

Notice for yourself what happens when you get attached to an outcome. Notice what you're focused on. You can reduce your attachment by putting your focus on listening, asking questions, and paying attention to performance. You can change your focus from being right to getting the best result.

People will know whether you're just giving lip service to appearing non-attached and open. I've seen managers who will stand up in front of a meeting and say, "I want your feedback. Let's look at what's possible. I want to hear your options for a solution." But they're not listening. They've already decided and aren't willing to be influenced, but they go through the motions because someone said they needed to listen to feedback. That's not listening. Listening actually includes considering what someone says.

When you're attached you usually won't be willing to hang out in the unknown for even five minutes to explore alternatives. You won't offer your idea as one possible solution; you'll drive toward your solution believing it is the best one. You'll stop listening when people are talking. You'll just wait for them to be quiet so they can listen to your solution. When you're attached you'll notice people will feel less and less free to talk to you because they notice their words don't have an impact.

You may also notice that you don't get true agreement when you are attached. Your attachment can produce resistance with the very people you need to enroll. They might say yes in the meeting and then go do what they were going to do anyway.

Letting Go By Including

What do you do when you notice that you or someone you live or work with is attached to an outcome? How do you diffuse it? Can you diffuse it? One thing is for sure: remain flexible—don't get attached to your idea. Otherwise you'll just polarize the conversation into an either/or scenario where no one can win. What you can say is, "Help me understand why you think this idea is the best one." And explore the merit of the idea independent of their attachment or their attitude.

I was in a brainstorming meeting when someone expressed an idea I found weak. While I was thinking about what to say, another manager responded by saying, "That has merit." And then he moved forward to explore the idea in depth. Instead of rejecting the idea, he included it with a simple acknowledging statement. I had a lot of respect for this particular manager and his statement shifted my focus to listening for the merit in the idea, rather than dismissing it out of hand before it could be explored.

If you want people to listen to you, to understand what you're saying, to explore what's possible, then lead the way by listening, understanding, and exploring.

Creating Non-Defensive Environments

1. Set up a mistake-free zone in your meetings and conversations.
2. Consciously suspend reaction so you can listen.
3. Recognize and let go of your attachment to an outcome.

These three practices for creating non-defensive environments require attention to what you say and how you say it. These practices refine your ability to notice the impact of your words. It brings to mind the old saying that it's not what you say; it's how you say it. I would take this a step further and remind you that it's not what you say; it's who you are being when you say it. You choose your state of being ... open, defensive, generous, close-minded, stubborn, grateful, angry, forgiving, frustrated, truthful, compassionate, phony, authentic, free or ... you fill in the blank. Who are you in this moment? Who you are speaks louder than words.

This practice of non-attachment comes with the understanding that you're not bound by conditions and you're not controlled by others' behavior. As you gain ground in this practice, people around you will learn that if they put an issue on the table you will ask questions, explore ideas, and get a commitment to take action in an agreed-upon time frame. This practice builds relationships and teams. Your spouse, partner, families, and co-workers will know they can talk to you about anything. If you're not attached you're free to act and your performance improves whether it's in sports, life, or on the job.

Your goal is to leave yourself and others fulfilled and in action to succeed. Replacing attachment with commitment brings you present to what you can do now.

Practice: *Notice when you get attached to an outcome. Examine how it impacts results, relationships, and your well-being.*

Change naturally occurs when you observe the impact of your behavior. It's at that moment you have the opportunity to wake up to what's effective and leave behind thinking, communication, and interactions that are not fulfilling for your spirit or getting the job done.

Chapter 10

Promises

"Half of the troubles in the world are from saying yes too quickly and the other half is from not saying no soon enough." Josh Billings

Fulfillment starts with a promise.

What is a promise? Have you ever heard a child ask, "You promise?" They look you in the eye and in the heart and you know you'll disappoint them if you waiver from your word. It is this simple understanding that forges our relationship with a promise. Not just the promises we make in the world, but also the promises we make to ourselves. The first promise inherent in all promises is the commitment to keep them. A promise is the beginning of a cycle of fulfillment. Broken promises generate a cycle of disappointment and diminish your own sense of trust and belief that you can do what you say you will do.

The dictionary tells us that a promise means "a declaration given by you that something will or will not be done."

This meaning tells us the power in a promise is the declaration that moves your words into action. When you take action to fulfill a promise, it unleashes the future achievement now.

Think about the promises you make today. Do you ever make a promise that you're not committed to keep? Would you actually say to yourself or someone else, in the moment of making the promise, "Yes, I'll do it if something better doesn't come along?" Or "Yes, I'll stick with my diet plan if no one offers me a cookie." Would you actually say those words out loud to someone else or even to yourself in a quiet moment? I don't think so. Yet in the moment when you give up on keeping your word, that's exactly what you're saying. You're saying, "I'm bound by conditions. If conditions aren't right I can't keep my promises." You're saying that something else (the cookie, the possibility of a better opportunity) is more important than keeping your word. This is a recipe for disappointment.

Why would any of us break our promises?

Most often when you look into why, you'll find out you had some doubts that you would do it in the first place. And you didn't express those doubts. Why wouldn't you pause and say no or tell the truth? I hear all kinds of reasons. "I didn't want to sound negative," "I didn't want to make them angry," "I didn't want to disappoint them." "I didn't have a choice, I couldn't say no." Whatever the reason, even when there's no one else involved, and you're making a promise to yourself, slow down and carefully consider what you're being asked to do. A promise is your word in action and is believable because you say so. It's a creative act.

It's essential in the practice of fulfillment to discover what you make more important than being your word and why that takes precedence. This discovery is facilitated by recognizing what you make more important—on a routine basis—than keeping your promise. If your commitment isn't about delivering on what you say you will do, you're already planning to break your word. Do the promises you make at work, at home and personally to yourself and others take on an urgent and important status in your daily actions?

Urgent and Important

Remember Stephen Covey's business grid that identifies tasks as important and urgent? It breaks it down into four parts:

Important and urgent.
Important and not urgent.
Not important and urgent.
Not important and not urgent.

The bottom line of this analysis says most people don't get to the "important and not urgent" elements of their job or life. Sound familiar? Fulfillment is important but may not be seen as urgent. Fulfillment is often seen as something you'll get around to in the future. Then the promises you make that aren't in the urgent category get pushed to the side.

However, sometimes (maybe more often than not) we are doing what's not important and not urgent ... those computer games, TV, endless chatter, sleeping in, escaping into books, food, or addiction ... instead of what you know your promises are calling you to do.

Who are you when you make a promise? Let's break the question down to look more closely. Who you are is what you bring to any promise ... your history, thoughts, habits, emotions, beliefs, and ideas. Are you automatically agreeing or making a promise because of the person asking? In business I've been asked, "What do you do if it's your boss asking?" I reply, "I don't automatically agree. I ask questions." If you automatically agree and then don't fulfill the promise, who is served? If you fulfill the promise and are resentful or feel taken advantage of, who is served? By asking questions, you can determine priorities. You can also inform your boss about the other initiatives you have scheduled. You get your boss's partnership to determine whether something needs to shift for you to take action and make a new promise.

You don't have to be automatic in your personal life either. You start to wake up and ask questions. You begin to say no when that's the authentic response. When you learn to say no, you can make a commitment and mean it, or you can negotiate an alternative. As you take on the practice of keeping your promises and being your word, just notice your thoughts, emotions, and what you say. Listen carefully. You don't have to do anything. Just notice what happens when you make a promise. What would you say about yourself? Notice whether the requirements to fulfill the promises you make are voiced or unexpressed. Is there any conversation with yourself or others, after the fact, about why you said yes and what yes means?

Do you ever give in and do something just because someone else wants you to agree, even though it will prevent you from keeping your original plan? If your answer is yes and you say you're happy to do it, it most likely doesn't show up as resignation or a "have-to." However if your commitment in other areas slips, question why you felt the need to say yes instead of respectfully declining. Or if the yes gets delivered with a deep sigh and a one-word response, like "okay" and gets done with regret, use the regret as a wakeup call to say no and reclaim the power of your word. Keep in mind what the definition of a promise is: it's the declaration to do something or not do something. You can say no with love.

People often forget that no is a commitment just like its

popular sibling, yes. Both yes and no are promises.

Now it may sound funny to say that no is a promise. Why is it a promise? It's a promise not to do something. No is what makes choice possible. No is what makes authentic commitment possible. It means after careful consideration I am committed or not committed to doing something in a given time frame.

If you say you'll do something, you'll find that if you don't, you carry the promise around like an incomplete action, an eternal "to do" list you don't get to. Or you might tell yourself that you meant to do it! That's the meaning of maybe. My children taught me early on as a parent not to say maybe. My daughter told me, "Mom, just say yes or no. Maybe doesn't mean anything." She was 16 years old at the time … pretty smart if you ask me. There's no commitment in a maybe.

There is power in saying no. If you can't say no, it's a forced choice; a "have to" where you assume no other possibility exists. Instead consider what's fulfilling and what you want to bring forward in the world.

The Power Of Your Word

The promise in fulfillment is you simply do what you say because you say so. In that way you build the power of your word. You begin to pay attention to the promises you do make. You give up the notion of being coerced into making promises. You give up pretending not to have a choice in the matter. You do have a choice. You begin to reflect on your calling, that slowly growing sense that something is urging you forward, and find out whether that is guiding your life instead of an endless stream of have-to's.

This practice of being your word brings you present. When you repeatedly have a list of broken promises, it fuels what's not complete and keeps you anchored in the past. There's a point when you have to let go and be complete so you can move forward. It's not aging that makes you old or burdened; it's a continual looking back with regret.

Questions To Ask Yourself

What are you committed to? If you find it hard to answer that question, look around in your life and day-to-day experience and you'll see the facts of the matter in what you do, day in and day out. That's what you're committed to!

Take a moment to reflect on the promises you've made. If you're not in action to fulfill the promise, ask yourself what you make more important than keeping your word to others or to yourself. No judgment, just notice. What do you make more important than being fulfilled?

Reflect on the simple practice of doing what you say just because you say so. This practice will bring you present and help create the space for you to discover the power of your word.

Practice: *Today only make promises you intend to keep and notice what happens to your conversations, your actions, your relationships, and your sense of fulfillment.*

The declaration "I am my word" is a key to fulfillment and is the power behind commitment that produces results.

Remember the story of the master and the overflowing teacup? I have listened to this story many times as a reflection on being so full of what we already know there's no room for any new learning, any enlightenment. Now I also chuckle when I hear it because it points to an additional insight of being so full of what I said I would do there's no room for ... well ... anything, let alone quiet inquiry, reflection on fulfillment, or careful consideration of saying yes to something new.

Fulfilled people manage by commitment and begin to realize the power in "yes." If you say yes, you have set up a course of action to complete. If your commitment "cup" is too full, there's no room for anything new. If you want to make a new commitment ask yourself what's incomplete and complete it. Then you'll find yourself in a clearing of your own creation where you can think about where you want to place your new promise. Place it carefully with fulfillment in mind.

Chapter 11

What Is Your Original Promise?

"Remember that you are unique. If that has not been fulfilled then something wonderful has been lost." Martha Graham

In 1979 I went to a retreat with three friends and for several days we focused on one inquiry. The purpose of the inquiry was to discover who you are. I sat among a group of about thirty people. One person at a time, we made a simple request of each other: "Tell me who you are." Then we listened to each other's answers. At the end of each session we thanked our partner and then rotated to another person. In between sessions, we had simple meals and did solitary walks, making the request internally with no judgment or blocking of any responses. We were instructed just to note the response, say a silent thank you, and continue the inquiry.

The responses were varied. Some people were firmly rooted in the physical and were uncomfortable with sitting or with silence for the length of time required. Some scorned the process as boring or a waste of time. Some moved into a point of detached amusement. Some continued to look a little deeper in each round of questions. I found answering the question from a place of true inquiry included frustration, delight, judgment, laughter, and irritation; and the experience transported me to a point where I was everything and nothing. It was a meditation that brought clarity, and in a way that's hard to explain, it also brought joy and peace of mind.

After what seemed like the sessions could go on forever, I realized there was no definitive answer just an endless opportunity to know myself and others. I also had a deepening awareness that I could create my life and experience unconditionally.

A thought that had nagged at me my whole life had settled in with a new sense of purpose. What I was called to do, what ignited my passion, now seemed both familiar and new. When I was quite young, I had an abrupt awakening. I grew up in a beautiful neighborhood and went to school with friends who had different religious backgrounds. On one occasion, I was walking home from grammar school with my friend and we were talking about graduating into 7th grade the following year. My friend was going to attend a private school and very matter of factly told me that people of my religion couldn't attend. When I asked her why she said she didn't know. So we promptly made a path to her house to ask her mom. I'll never forget her mom's response to our eager questions of why I couldn't attend. She said, "Let's go have ice cream!" never answering the question. The look on her face, however, spoke volumes. My parents confirmed that I couldn't attend and began a conversation about intolerance and prejudice.

My parents had different religious backgrounds. My mom was the "right" religion for the school but my father's religion was excluded. I loved my mom and my dad so it wouldn't work for me to make a religion wrong for the acts of some of its people.

I started to think about how to speak and listen to each other so we could reach past prejudices and exist with compassion for differences. We could replace judgment with curiosity. We could even move past tolerating each other and expand into appreciating each other.

I began to wonder whether we could look into our own pre-conceived notions of who we are and determine where they originated. Could we recognize the possibility that our pre-conceived notions may be interpretations based on where we were born and the culture we were born into? Could we notice when these notions became behavioral imperatives for separation and an integral part of who we are before we were even aware of them?

Is it possible to explore something truly original that hasn't been passed on to you as a way to be? First you'd have to reflect on who you have been up until now and think about how you currently define yourself. Most often you don't question who you are until you notice that something is missing in your life.

The inquiry "tell me who you are" is powerful. It unfolds layers and layers of what you think you are. As you expose those layers and continue to inquire, something is revealed that may be yet unformed. You may be left with the idea that who you are in the world is somehow fundamentally different from how you see yourself living your life as a fulfilled human being. Major life events, a nagging dissatisfaction or disappointment can fuel the question, "What am I doing with my life?" You don't have to wait for something to happen to fuel this kind of inquiry.

As I continued to explore I became aware of a new question … a question that brought me full circle, back to my early awakening. "What is your original promise?" As I contemplated this new question, I felt the pulse of the inquiry … a pull to respond to a call and to start now.

Your original promise is not what you do when you're

not working or when you have time.

Your original promise is fundamentally the reconciliation of who you are and what you do.

You can use the question about your original promise to access what often lays hidden away for some future time when financial goals or obligations are complete. What was your intention earlier in life? What was it that you wanted to accomplish? What were you passionate about?

I was speaking at a conference where we had a lively discussion about the idea of having an original promise. One of the participants asked me to define "original promise." I found myself talking around it and not wanting to define it. Original means created directly and personally, not an imitation. Promise means a vow, a calling. Revealing your original promise is a quest not an answer. What I've found so far is that your original promise is an inner calling that guides you and lets you know when you're on course and when you're off course.

"I think most of us are looking for a calling not a job. Most of us have jobs that are too small for our spirit. Jobs are not big enough for people." This was said by Nora Watson in Studs Terkel's *Working* published in 1974. This is as true today as it was then. We have become more productive with technology and innovation but still fulfillment and meaning are elusive if the promise of who we are is unrealized.

Your original promise is calling you. It's the voice you can't ignore. It's your inner guidance. It's your higher self. It may be accessed through mindfulness, inquiry, and intuition. I call it your original promise because it will keep nudging you. It's like trying to solve the mystery of who you are: you sit, open up, let go of conditioned thinking, and allow understanding to emerge.

You may have to unlearn some routines, behaviors, and ways of being that no longer serve you. The core of fulfillment is not ego, fantasy, or image-driven. The core of fulfillment is to be present and connect with what's possible now.

You may notice that on the job or on the world stage we continue to talk about thinking outside the box, but in actuality, we rarely stray from our historical ways of dealing with life and people. If we did, we would more rapidly learn from history rather than continue to travel the same path time and time again; a path that doesn't produce fulfillment personally or globally.

I believe that well-aimed questions can access an awakened state of being, an alignment of who you are in action in the world. You begin to recognize your connection to everyone. You start to operate differently in your daily practices. And the result? You wake up to what's possible for you and the world you live in ... for you and for all of us.

The question "What is your original promise?" is designed for insightful reflection. Your response will impact how you show up in the world. This question is designed to quiet your mind and allow your purpose, your calling—that which fulfills you—to be seen and heard. And when you know it, you know it like a deep breath of fresh air, a slowly growing awareness enveloping you with no attachment, just a sense of gratitude for who you are. And then naturally you bring that authentic you into your daily practice. You bring that practice to what you are doing today, right where you are ... in your communication and on your job. You don't have to live a separate life, one way at work and another way at home.

When work comes from your original promise, it's fulfilling. It's not something you do on the way to being fulfilled. With this dawning realization you can begin to see a golden thread of fulfillment connecting events in your life when guided by your original promise.

What would you say is your original promise?

My original promise is to speak the truth with love and to act from connection instead of reacting from separation ... to replace violence in thoughts, words, and actions with respectful dialogue and negotiation. Remember what Rumi said, "A moment of patience instead of anger prevents a thousand days of sorrow." When my actions are infused with my original promise, there's no residue, nothing to clean up later. My original promise is a way of being that gives meaning to my work, my relationships, and my life—it's not that I don't get angry, judgmental or impatient, I do. My practice is not to act on it. I recognize the balance and continued insights that come from practice. I'm not waiting for fulfillment. When it's missing I know it's missing and the opportunity is ever-present to bring it to what is happening now.

One of my dear friends told me recently about an experience that caused her to remember an idea she's carried around since childhood. She asked me what would it be like if all children everywhere were given the opportunity to learn, thrive, and feel safe? It became clear that it was time for her to get involved, to take up the challenge and set the leader in her free. She was animated in ways I hadn't seen before. She immediately embraced the challenge and joined a project to help build an eco-birthing center in Uganda and provide training for midwives to reduce the mortality rate for mothers and newborns; and to work with the local community to build schools that include a sustainable farm to feed the children and teachers. As I was listening to her, I knew she was making contact with her original promise.

Questions To Think About

1. What are you called to do?

2. What activates fulfillment for you?

3. What are you grateful for in your life?

4. What nourishes your spirit?

5. What is the difference you make right where you are?

6. If you set the leader in you free to think, what would you know? If you set the leader in you free to speak, what would you hear? If you set the leader in you free to act, what would you do?

7. What is your original promise? (You may find a clue to your original promise in inquiring into what ignites your passion.)

Practice: *Take some quiet time to reflect on the question, "Tell me who you are," as if you were sitting in front of a mirror asking yourself the question. What would you say in response?*

Your practice is to notice with curiosity and interest without judgment or attachment. Ask yourself throughout the day what you notice about who you are in any situation you find yourself.

Pay attention as you go through your day at work, at home, or at play, and notice if "who you are" is reconciled with what you do. Notice if there are any gaps and what might bring them into balance.

Chapter 12

Finding Fulfillment Where You Are

"A little less conversation, a little more action please." Elvis Presley

I've heard reports that when people get close to death and are asked what they would've done differently, they often say they would have taken more risks. They also say they would work less and spend more time with family. That may be easier to say on reflection than to actually take risks now or make a change in work today. If you're going to do something new or think in new ways, you need a blend of pragmatism and risk taking. Sometimes a great achievement for you will start with a sacrifice. The sacrifice is fulfilling because it moves you toward achieving what you say will make you, and others, happy. Sacrifice is also hard because you may have to give up some cherished notions or beliefs or some comfortable old habits or routines. What makes taking a risk worthwhile?

Conduct your own survey. Ask people if they are satisfied in their current jobs. Many say they're looking for an opportunity where they can make a difference or be successful; where they are happy to be at work or can achieve a work/life balance. Reflect on the question yourself. What I find in my conversations with people on the job is often a pattern of non-fulfillment in the workplace. Winning the game at work and being fulfilled are not mutually exclusive.

Do you notice that you never ask yourself the question, "What am I doing here?" when you're fulfilled? When you're operating from fulfillment you disappear into the action. You are satisfied that you are moving toward your intended result even when there's a problem.

In business, we ask people to take accountability for producing intended results. What do we ask for in relationships? We ask for love, understanding, and accountability. We ask each other to take accountability for what is occurring in our lives and in our relationships ... now. Accountability is essential to finding fulfillment where you are.

The shift to accountability requires knowing your vision and goals whether it's on the job or in a relationship.

If you ask people to own the goals, you are also asking whether they're ready, willing, and able ... you are asking them to fulfill the goals with their heart and soul. If you are asking anyone else for that kind of commitment, it also needs to exist in you. If that's missing in you, where does the passion, leadership, and extraordinary action live? If you're coaching others as a business associate, program leader, or manager and you're not fulfilled, it shows. At the end of the day people don't work for companies, they work for people. They want to be inspired.

Accomplished leaders know that people do not consistently perform at high levels if they're not doing the things they really want to do. So they want to know something about their team members' vision and values in order that the goals they take on are infused with a sense of purpose. They inspire their players to be on the field playing full out, knowing they are developing their team to achieve the life skills necessary to fulfill anything both personally and professionally.

Here's something I've learned over the last 25 years as

a business leader. It was my vision to have an organization that was dedicated to transforming people's lives and businesses, so my husband and I started a company called Empowerment Technology Corporation. We focused on developing a training program called *On Course* that was attended by thousands of people from all walks of life. *On Course*, a personal effectiveness program, taught three key practices: accountability, non-attachment, and commitment. Subsequently, organizations would bring us in to help them teach their teams how to talk to each other, achieve goals, and resolve conflict. My practice extended for fifteen years coaching performance and resolving conflict. And then something unexpected occurred.

Our friend Wally Arnold called to invite us to start a new company. He described the concept as an antidote to the fast-paced, technological, stressed environment in which many people find themselves living. He had a vision of people coming home and lighting candles and in that simple act would take a moment and create an ambiance for relaxation, romance, rituals, and reflection. This candle company would put me on the playing field to actually do all the things I was teaching. It wasn't too long after I started working at this new company, Illuminations, that I called many of my former clients and let them know how hard it was to actually take 100% accountability, let go of attachment to an outcome, produce intended results, and stay committed over time. We laughed and laughed. I saw daily that human beings blame first, are loath to "inquire within," refuse to notice their attachments (especially to being right), and see commitment as a strain on their freedom.

I recognized early on at Illuminations that the game was to interrupt performance-limiting beliefs and break out to a new level of performance that produced results and fulfillment.

When my husband and I joined our friend Wally to start this new enterprise, I noticed several things. First, there is energy around start-ups, around beginnings where possibilities seem limitless. Start-ups are an act of creation. Something that does not exist has the potential to exist. Entrepreneurs are people who have mastered the art of creation; Wally is an entrepreneur extraordinaire.

What I've noticed over the years is that people want to be around visionary leaders, because they see more possibilities in life and business. This is especially true when there are setbacks. Leaders know that setbacks inform the new action that needs to happen.

This was illustrated daily at Illuminations. This business had more unexpected setbacks than any other business I've been part of. Some of these were major setbacks. Wally left the day-to-day business. There were many management changes, new strategies tried, infusions of capital, a Chapter 11 reorganization, but nothing seemed to recapture the promise that existed at the beginning. Then the board asked Wally to come back when it was clear that his declaration of stewardship over the Illuminations' brand was not complete. As soon as he returned, although three years had gone by, the excitement started to rebuild. We brought in some new players. We designed a new store and, within five months of the conception of the idea, we opened the new prototype. We had to find a location, negotiate the deal, sign leases, engage an architect and general contractor, deal with permits and inspections, and be open before the holidays! It seemed impossible. We were closing stores, not opening stores, but once the vision was clear and the actions were planned, including dealing with the obstacles that would—and did—arise, everything fell into place. We opened on time and a new company vision was born. A store rollout was planned, a new buying team was hired, and subsequently the company caught the attention of a national retailer and was sold within fifteen months.

What happened, or more interestingly, what was missing that caused the company to languish after a skyrocketing beginning? Was it macroeconomic reasons ... softening economy, dot.com bust, more competition, increased costs of raw materials, or was it internal reasons ... a focus on growing too fast and not enough focus on the bottom line? A forward-looking vision and strategy was missing that would create a reason for growing the business starting where we were, instead of where we thought we were going to be.

The truth is that without a vision, people don't know where they're going or how they can make a contribution. They don't know what to be committed to or how to be fulfilled. As a leader you must be able to speak to the vision as it is today and communicate that in a way that inspires action. You can downsize, cut costs, trim overhead, increase margins, and still you need a reason for being. Vision is the organizing principle that draws people together. It was vision that created Illuminations in the first place. Illuminations' original promise was to inspire people to live every day by candlelight and in doing so, transform their lives and homes. It wasn't that anyone else didn't try during the troubled years, they did. We all did. But the actions didn't steer off the vision of the company and so became a string of hits and misses without a unique reason for being. Visionary leaders are priceless. They create brands that foster loyalty by connecting to their customers and employees for life, and rewarding them both in tangible and intangible ways.

What Is Your Vision Of A Life Worth Living?

Your fulfillment has its roots in vision, a vision that organizes your actions time after time. What do you want to create? The good news is you already have a vision. Look at what is around you right now and it will reveal your vision of what's possible. If it's not what you want, reflect on your original promise and let that guide you. Maybe it's time to create a new vision, one that reflects your original promise. Remember that your vision is so because you say so. Once you declare your vision, you start planning and taking action.

What can you do right now that is in alignment with your vision? Can you stop doing what's not fulfilling? You know what's not fulfilling. It's what you regret with the benefit of hindsight; it's often the regret in the next 24 hours! After you exercise do you ever say, "Why did I do that?" Most likely you say, "Glad I did that!" You don't regret what is fulfilling, even when it's hard to do.

There is an old Zen story: "On the way to being fulfilled, be fulfilled." Well, actually the story is "Riding an ox, looking for an ox." We're looking for what we don't have and forget that it's available right here and right now. Fulfillment is here, it's possible. You can find fulfillment where you are if you bring the qualities of what you're looking for to what you are currently doing.

I have a friend who is not happy in her job. She tells me the people she works with complain and don't have a high sense of integrity. I asked her how she is responding to these conditions at work. She reflected that she just silently judges her co-workers and wishes she were somewhere else. Her resume shows her jumping from job to job every 18 months. I asked her how she would grade her integrity on the job, and if she had to stay in the job (no exit possible), what could she do? It didn't take her long to realize that she could move from silence to telling the truth (lead by example) and when others complain she could find out what they wanted, so they could make a request or take action and end the complaint. Is the risk worth taking? It surprises me how often people would rather leave than confront the issues and practice living a fulfilled life versus continuing to complain about life.

I don't advocate staying in an environment that is not fulfilling. I also don't advocate leaving because others aren't living up to your "ideal" of how they should be when you aren't living up to it either. Consider staying where you are and starting to practice living your vision of fulfillment where you are. You may find out that what you're looking for is already there.

When you make that shift, you realize that you are accountable for your fulfillment and you stop waiting for someone else or a new job or some new condition to provide what only you can make happen.

Practice: *Take some time and think about what fulfillment means to you. Write in a journal, muse when you're drinking your coffee, or taking a leisurely walk. Take a 5 minute break out of your busy day to sit and contemplate the question.*

Write down what you want, along with a statement that declares why it will bring fulfillment and meaning to your life. Through this practice you will begin to shape your vision of a life worth living.

To whom can you declare your vision? Find someone who can be a committed partner or coach for you. This can help you clarify and breathe life into your vision and will help you stay on course.

Once you declare your vision, you can define what action you will take that brings sustainable fulfillment ... not sometime in the future, but in the actions you take right now.

Chapter 13

Breakdowns Into Breakthroughs

"The pessimist sees difficulty in every opportunity. The optimist sees the opportunity in every difficulty." Winston Churchill

If you're at this point in reading *The Promise Of Fulfillment* you probably have an inkling of your original promise and your vision of a life worth living. This is a good place to discuss potential breakdowns in case they might stop you from ever getting started beyond imagining what you want.

What happens if you run into some obstacles? Some of those obstacles may be easier to anticipate and plan for, but others may be unexpected. Your vision must be strong enough to include the potential problems and obstacles that happen along the way. Otherwise those self-limiting stories that tell a tale about why it can't be done start to emerge.

What you can do is set up a process to implement when breakdowns happen. This is like having the "Break Glass In Case Of Fire" sign in your building. You're not planning on a fire, but just in case, you have a fire extinguisher and even a way to communicate to the fire department.

Anticipating Breakdowns

What do you do with your goals when you have a breakdown? Ask yourself the following three questions before something happens so you can be prepared and also so you can discover something about how you function around breakdowns:

1. What do you notice about yourself when you have a problem, obstacle, or challenge to achieving what you want?
2. If your answer is it depends on the problem, in what areas are you effective and when are you ineffective?
3. What do you say to yourself and others when you solve the problem and what do you say to yourself and others when you don't?

Some people tell me breakdowns are a sign to stop. Breakdowns are not a sign to stop. Breakdowns happen. Breakdowns interrupt the action and are a sign to pay attention. Some people want to hide the breakdown because they don't want to look bad.

Breakdowns reveal your commitment.

Some people stop completely, are continually disappointed, and don't even look at what's possible. Thus the idea that they could live a fulfilled life goes south in a hurry. Other people tell me breakdowns are part of the process of getting things done. Still, others will say that it depends on the breakdown! Is it at work, no problem … in relationships, big problem.

Breakdowns may challenge your ability and your resources but don't let them challenge your willingness to deal with them. Breakdowns stop the action; they don't stop you or turn off your commitment. Only you can do that. Breakdowns are powerful when confronted because it gives you the opportunity to assess what's working and what isn't working. This is the time to ask for feedback, notice what's missing, ask questions, and improve your plan. You may have to take new action, shift strategies, or ask for help to get the results you want.

Don't hide breakdowns or obstacles. Expose them! Declare any breakdown in your plan of action to your committed partners, and actively look for what's possible and handle it early. Don't gloss over breakdowns. They often contain the seeds of profound breakthroughs when discovered early. Left unattended they can fester and drastically alter the course of the plan.

When you follow up regularly on the actions you and others take, you'll be likely to predict or catch breakdowns before they occur. Breakdowns and obstacles, when addressed, make people smarter and stronger. The following is one of my personal mantras: turn breakdowns into breakthroughs.

This mantra reminds me to pay attention and not stop because there's a block to my progress. I've learned that progress is not automatic. You have to deal with what shows up.

This is one of my favorite breakdown stories. Do you know how Post-it notes were invented? Someone designed glue that didn't stick completely. It didn't do what it was designed for. But it did something else. It allowed papers to stick together long enough so that someone could peel off a paper one at a time. That breakdown turned into a breakthrough. Now they're indispensable and come in different sizes and colors. We have fax Post-it notes and for-your-information Post-it notes, some personalized Post-it notes. We even have message Post-it notes. [Post-it® notes is a registered trademark of 3M Company.]

The point is obstacles and breakdowns are part of the process of accomplishment. They're not to be avoided; they're meant to be faced.

The Power In A Breakdown

The power in breakdowns is the opportunity to have something new revealed. It might be a new product or a new goal; or it might be a new strategy to achieve your original goal. It might be a stronger team or relationship.

At the beginning of one year my assistant had a great idea to turn our weekly meeting into a celebration of the new year. She created postcards with one new year's resolution printed on each card and spread them all over the buffet table for a company breakfast meeting. She thought it would be great fun to have a New Year's Resolution Breakfast with healthy food. If you think about it, you may notice that resolutions come out of noticeable breakdowns! I walked around the table and read each one out loud:

Lose weight.
Make more money.
Get out of debt.
Pay off credit cards.
Stop smoking.
Stop drinking.
Have more fun.
Get a relationship.
Go to the gym.
Start exercising.
Spend more time with family.
Stop gossiping.

Get promoted.
Spend more time outdoors.
Get more education.
Save money.

Feel free to add your favorite resolutions to the list. Everyone at the meeting laughed and yelled out any resolutions that were missing for them. These are all the familiar *have to* statements that are talked about year after year. If you're saying "Yeah" to any of these, most likely you're engaged in some activity that continues to fuel the breakdown and the need for a resolution. You may think that if you lose the weight, get the relationship, run the marathon, get the promotion, or have the time, then you will be fulfilled. You're waiting to have the experience of being fulfilled once you get what you want.

Think about every time you set a goal to lose weight, get out of debt, spend more time with your family, exercise, or just have time to relax and breathe. These are popular New Year's resolutions that are set year after year. The question is how do you turn the breakdown (high blood pressure, stress, weight gain, high cholesterol, no time) into a breakthrough (health, clear energy, feeling great, looking good, family time).

My husband and I keep Saturdays as special days just to be together. One Saturday morning we were picking up our car from the dealer, waiting for them to fix one more thing. It took longer than expected so we just stood there talking about what we talk about when there's no pressure of goals, work, and timelines. We talked about what we were going to do that day and didn't come up with any plan, just a lot of "maybe this" or "maybe that" ideas. My husband stepped away for a moment to check on the progress of the car and instead of thinking about what we could do, I thought about what would be fulfilling to do. I could easily fast-forward to après event to know whether I was leaning in the direction of fulfillment. It was so simple. When my husband returned from his conversation with the mechanics, I was already fulfilled and shared with him my aha moment. We both set off, car fixed, to have a glorious run, yoga, and lunch … laughing all the way. It was only a quirk of a moment—looking at alternatives through the prism of fulfillment versus the prism of habit. Imagine if you used that prism to look at work, health, relationships, and fun!

Now imagine if you used the prism of fulfillment to look at breakdowns and problems.

You'll notice that you will achieve what you want if you don't let breakdowns stop you. They are momentary setbacks along the way. The way you stay on course is to revisit your original vision and promise, then lead from what inspired you in the first place. Your vision organizes your actions moment to moment and the breakdowns you experience become great strength-building stories to tell later on. Overcoming obstacles is part of what makes you great. Remember the chapter on high participation and low attachment? You let go of the concern about the obstacle and up the ante on your commitment to the goal. You stay engaged. If your New Year's resolution is in alignment with your vision of a life worth living, it's possible to achieve! If not, it's wishful thinking.

Think about the true stories that inspire you the most. I'd guess they are stories about people who met impossible odds and achieved their goals. I think about the running story related in *Chariots of Fire* when Eric Liddell was knocked to the ground several strides into the race. He paused, got up, and went after his competitors, who were by then well ahead. He caught the leaders and crossed the finish line first. When he fell, it looked like he was out of the race. Instead he picked himself up and kept running. He won the race. It reminds me that no matter how many times you fall down you have to keep getting back up.

I coach people every day who add extra concern to the obstacles they're facing. When I help them eliminate the concern (and their self-limiting story), we're left to face the facts and fix the problem. Usually the concern is mired in how they're going to appear to others.

Get upset with yourself or others later. Fix the problem first. Then remember that what you can access is a greater generosity of spirit, rather than making others wrong for "knocking you to the ground" or making yourself wrong for what you did or didn't do.

Turn your breakdown into a coaching moment.

Declare the breakdown and use all your resources to turn it into a breakthrough. Stay on the field of action rather than be a spectator in the stands yelling insults. Change your behavior on the field of action and you change your results not in the future, but right now.

Practice: *Don't waste a breakdown. You'll find your stamina and resourcefulness increase when you don't give up. Ask for help if you need it. Acknowledge mistakes and get the information you need to break through to the solution.*

Remember take one step at a time with focus and attention. This builds your fulfillment practice. Let go of any attachment to the outcome and bring your attention present to this moment. The way to break through is to get back on the field of action and find the solution by facing the obstacle. The way to win is to keep playing. If you give up, you automatically lose.

Play the game with accountability, love, and commitment—the fundamental qualities of fulfillment.

Chapter 14

Finding Fulfillment In Conflict

"How can I be so right and be so wrong!" Michael Sun

Nothing can derail fulfillment faster than conflict. I remind myself when conflict occurs that it's the beginning of a resolution process and the work is to find a solution that can serve all the participants' interests. I keep that in mind as I work through the issues, even when it's a legal matter. I also remind myself that conflict is natural, it's part of the process of getting things done and it's part of the process of living!

What does the word "conflict" conjure up in your mind? Is it confrontation, arguments, avoidance, shutting down, escape, or is it an opportunity? Who are you around conflict or even potential conflict? What do you notice about your behavior and your communication? When there is conflict, what is your way of dealing with it?

1. Do you handle it when it first shows up?
2. Or do you avoid it?
3. Do you attack?
4. Or do you defend?
5. Do you play nice, hoping everyone will just calm down and the conflict will go away?
6. Or is it a "my way or the highway" kind of approach where you have to win regardless of the cost?

It's important to recognize your habitual way of dealing with conflict when it doesn't resolve successfully. Keep your habits in mind as you read through these ideas on conflict resolution so you can recognize your learning edge. You may find you do some combination of these strategies depending on the person or the situation.

One way you can access how you operate around conflict is to listen to what you say to yourself and others about it. Do you have a limiting story about conflict or confrontation? When I've asked that question in trainings and management meetings just about everyone's hand in the room goes up. What's their limiting story? It's a variation on the theme: "This should not be happening to me!"

Conflict Is Part Of Life

I'm offering a different way of thinking about conflict and a different approach: Conflict will happen. Conflicts are like problems; everyone has them, no one wants them. I think the challenge is that most people haven't been trained to resolve conflict without killing (figuratively and literally) the other person. The idea is to confront conflict when it first occurs, so it doesn't escalate, whether in your personal life or in your business life. Confront may be a strong word. I'm using it intentionally given its meaning—"to face up to or deal with". You can confront without being confrontational. If you're reluctant to confront, what stops you? What do you tell yourself will happen if you confront the person?

Take some time to think about this. Is there any conflict you're currently involved in or perhaps experienced recently that's still hanging around? The way you'll know it's hanging around is that you still have conversations about it with yourself or other people. Think about a recent conflict you've experienced. What do you say about the people involved? What is it based on? And does what you say move you and others forward to resolution? Or does what you say move you toward a more entrenched notion of being right? Do you have limiting stories about the people involved? Are you telling yourself that if they were just more enlightened they would see your point of view?

I have a question for you: in these situations would you rather be right or resolved? If you answer that you'd rather be right, go back and re-read the chapter on letting go of attachment (Letting Go Without Giving Up) and then continue!

If you want resolution, you must first recognize and intervene in your own limiting stories about the situation. These stories will sound like blame, excuses, revenge, defense, and justifications. They replace any new thoughts, words, or actions that could resolve the conflict. These are the limiting stories you tell (or accept from others) that don't do anything except continue to perpetuate the conflict. These stories keep you from taking relevant action now, and prevent you from being fulfilled now.

You have the opportunity to be fulfilled in the process as well as in the resolution. The resolution practice that I will outline here helps you become aware of what you say and do that limits you, and what you say and do that fulfills you. It's easier on everyone, including yourself, if you give up your attachment to being right about the situation or any one solution. You don't have to give up on the solution you have in mind. Just let it be one of the possibilities. Do you know the difference? If you're attached to being right you won't listen to any other idea. If your idea is one of many and is the best solution, let the validity of your idea prevail.

Resolution doesn't mean getting your own way; it means you engage in discovering an outcome that works for all parties. You can stop arguing and start asking questions. Be inquisitive. Be interested. Be open.

Questions You Can Ask

- What happened?
- What's possible now?
- What do you want the future to look like?
- What do others want?
- What interests need to be served?
- What is your request?
- What are the other party's requests?
- What is the intention that needs to be fulfilled?
- What actions can all parties take to resolve this issue?
- What's required for you to be complete?
- What's required to prevent this from happening in the future?

Keeping an open mind is hard work. You know this is true if you've ever been on jury duty and the judge directs you to keep an open mind. What does it mean to keep an open mind? It means to not come to a conclusion until you hear all the evidence even if one side is compelling in their argument. The judge tells you that the evidence is not the arguments that the opposing sides give for your agreement but only those facts accepted as evidence by the court. In order to stay open when I was on jury duty, I had to face the myriad of conclusions that I'd already come to by the time I was seated on the jury, and let them go. I had to notice my bias, strip away seeking evidence that supported my bias, and give up like/dislike as a basis to decide. It was a phenomenal opportunity to practice being open-minded and also to understand how biased we are and how that impacts resolving conflict.

How do you openly inquire and listen to the responses to your questions? How can you actually be open-minded? One way is to listen to what's being said as a possibility. That it *may be* possible, rather than deciding in advance that it *is* possible or it *isn't* possible. If you think it is possible, you end the inquiry and if you think it's not possible you also end the inquiry. Both approaches will shut down any further conversation that is outside of what is either for or against the idea. Instead understand your bias and don't let it stop you from continuing the dialogue and discussion until a true resolution is created.

Practice: *Your practice in conflict situations is to generate agreement that resolution is possible. The first person to generate agreement with is yourself. Then you can get agreement with others. What's required for you to be committed to resolution?*

There may be no solution apparent at the beginning, just your commitment to resolution. This is an important distinction. A commitment to resolution allows you to stay in the conversation long enough to find, create, or uncover a way out of the conflict. Your willingness to have a dialogue and discussion is an example of a commitment to resolution. Mediation and coaching are also examples. Finding the fulfillment in conflict starts with your commitment to resolution.

Chapter 15

Separating Problems From Conflict

"Where all think alike, no one thinks very much." Walter Lipman

The first step in finding the fulfillment in conflict is to generate a commitment to resolution and stop waiting for the other person to be committed to resolution before you commit. You face the conflict and consider being more committed to resolution than having the conflict remain. A solution often comes out of this commitment to resolution and may be different and more creative than any individual would have thought when participants first encountered the conflict. A commitment to resolution allows honest dialogue and discussion, passion and position, intention and goals—it's an and/both proposition that invites the possibility of a sustainable solution.

You can start this practice by looking into where you create unnecessary conflict. I worked with a senior executive who created conflict whenever he got feedback until no one wanted to give him feedback. His mode of behavior was to attack. He realized he was getting a reputation that wouldn't serve him given his career goals. The funny thing is if you confronted him with facts unemotionally, he would reconsider—not easily however. Many people didn't think it was worth the energy it took to get him to change his mind, even when a different solution would work more easily than his. He had to win. His learning edge was to listen and consider ideas that weren't his. It was hard. He would rather be right than commit to resolution. This impacted his career and his relationships.

I worked with another executive who had the same issue, but a different response. She knew her strategy of "attack and defend" when listening to feedback didn't work and asked how she could suspend her initial reaction, so she could be committed to resolution and not create the conflict in the first place. So I created the "thank you moment." She committed to me that whenever she got feedback she would just say thank you. The response was immediately noticeable. When she said thank you she bought herself some time to digest the information, get some perspective, and get back to the person with clarifying questions, possible solutions, or a plan of action. It got to the point where she could say thank you and immediately move into the resolution process.

If you want other people to get in line with your ideas, be open to their ideas. It's the golden rule in action. You'll find that you discover more, build relationships that work, and resolve conflict more easily.

Identify The Underlying Problem

Essential to a commitment to resolution is developing the ability to distinguish the underlying problem from the conflict. What's the difference between problems and conflict? Think about it this way: when you set out to fulfill your promise or accomplish a goal you will have problems to solve. A customer isn't happy. You missed a deadline. A product didn't get designed. The product that got designed didn't work according to specifications. You ran out of money. You double-faulted your serve or missed your putt. Your strategy didn't work. You ate the whole cake! These are problems to be solved and you can find solutions. You may have to look at how to get more resources to accomplish the goal, how to correct the design, how to get the product to work, how to save money or shorten the time frame, or how to make the customer happy or improve your game. Or it may be that you just need to get back on track with your plan.

I look at conflict as something different from a problem to be solved. Conflict surrounds a problem. And sustained conflict can keep a problem from being faced and solved. Conflict occurs when individuals or groups don't get what they wanted, expected, or thought was fair. Look behind a conflict and you will find a complaint, a clash of expectations, values, or styles, a collision of ideas.

Ending A Tug Of War

Think about a tug of war. In a tug of war you have two positions—one at either end of a rope. The way you sustain a tug of war is for both people to keep tugging on their positions. Another way to say that is if two people get entrenched in their positions and both are attached to being right about the way things and people should be, their communication could be like a tug of war. And what happens in a tug of war? You exert force to pull people over to your side and then the other side exerts more force to pull you over to their side. When I ask people what they want in a conflict situation they'll tell me they want to get their point across. They want to be listened to, understood, and considered.

However if you could listen in to what someone is saying internally when conflict is happening it probably wouldn't be "I want to be understood." It would probably be more like "I'm right and you're wrong!"

Holding tightly to your position or focusing on being

right about your point escalates conflict. What happens if one person or a group of people put down the rope? The tug of war ends. What happens if you are willing to see your position as one possibility among several rather than holding on to being right? Is it possible to focus on solving the problem rather than being in conflict with another person or forcing a process that produces a winner and a loser? I think most conflicts can be resolved if people are aware of what the conflict is about (styles, expectations, or values), what keeps the conflict in place, and what the underlying problem is they need to resolve.

Can you find fulfilling solutions that resolve conflict? I believe you can and you must. Otherwise the solutions are short lived. What do you think keeps most conflict in place? Stories! Limiting stories based on evidence from the past. In conflict situations there's an intense focus on gathering evidence from the past that proves a fixed point of view.

Strong limiting stories prevent people from having a vision of the future that is different from the past. The result of this kind of thinking produces the idea that the future is going to be a replication of what's occurred in the past. So you get sidetracked from solving problems, and get more entrenched in the conflict, and then life becomes about getting even and making someone else miserable, making them wrong, or taking all you can with no regard for the other person. It's all about me and mine instead of all of us. It's the antithesis of fulfillment.

When you're having a conflict or you have a role in resolving the conflict, it's important to find out what the conflict is really about. Is it an unmet expectation? Is it a clash of styles or a collision of values? What are you dealing with?

Conflict Of Styles

When you realize your reaction to someone's style is creating the conflict, you can look at how to work with that particular style more effectively. You begin to realize the person is not out to get you! They are being who they are. You begin a process of discovery to find how to motivate, lead, be in a relationship with, or work for someone who has a different style from you. Behavioral, leadership, and communication style workshops can help you understand the basic differences in how people operate.

Styles can be predicted and understood. You don't have to look further than your own life to see that you and others around you have certain prescribed, favorite ways of approaching tasks and forming relationships. Think about the times when someone's action is so foreign to your way of thinking that truly you scratch your head and ask, "How could they say that?" Or "How can they be so disorganized? I could never be like that!" Or "How could they be so mean? I would never hurt someone's feelings." Or "How come it takes them so long to make a decision? Just decide!" Our examination usually goes no further unless there's conflict, and if left unchecked it can create great misunderstandings at work, in partnerships, marriage, and communities. One of the most commonly heard complaints in relationships is that the other person does not understand. This is the banner cry of a conflict of styles.

If it's a conflict of styles, it's critical to separate the people from the problem. There is a problem to be solved. Identify it. The dictionary defines a problem as any question or matter involving doubt, uncertainty, or difficulty. It's defined as a question proposed for a solution or discussion; synonyms for problems are puzzles, riddles, and enigmas. Sometimes a conflict of styles can seem like an enigma since someone else can appear so difficult for you. Consider that their style may be very different from yours and you don't have to make the other people or their style wrong. Identify the style so you can learn something about what they consider important.

The limiting stories we tell about other people are not the problem to be solved. However, those limiting stories can and do hold the conflict in place. Some stories are more entrenched than others, depending on the amount of history you have in telling and retelling the story about the conflict. There is a simple truth that is very challenging for people to live day-to-day: You can't change the past, but you can move on and shift your interpretation of what occurred and the meaning you give it.

You can look at the past as an accumulation of lessons learned and events that happened. It's important to recognize the past may hold some people in bondage. What do I mean by bondage? Revenge, being a victim, getting even. Being bound by the past means the past is using you instead of you using whatever happened to wake up and be more effective. When this kind of thinking occurs, the focus is on defeating the person instead of the problem. If you put the past aside you have the opportunity to see things as they are now; this opens a space to discover what needs to be learned from the conflict, including how to work more effectively with different styles.

Conflict Of Expectations

Think about the times when you expect something you don't get from your relationships. Now maybe you expect your husband or wife, partner, or loved one to make dinner because they get home earlier than you. Only they don't make dinner. What happens? Do you get upset? And the other person wonders what's going on with you? One could ask, "Hmmm … well, why don't you just ask them to make dinner?" and the response is, "Well I shouldn't have to ask them, it's obvious." The only thing that's obvious is you think they should read your mind. That's what expectations do. They cause you to think that somebody should just know what you want them to do and how you want them to be. Remember, when you ask, you get a response—a yes or a no—that's a promise and a commitment.

I think the reason we like expectations is we don't have to ask. And if we don't have to ask, we don't have to confront a possible no or a possible discussion. I don't know about you but I grew up hearing the statement, "I don't want to discuss it." Well, sometimes we grow into adults and say the same thing to others. These same people who don't want to "discuss it" might be surprised why the people around them don't tell them the truth. Most of the people I talk to want the truth and wish people would just tell them the truth, but you have to be able to listen to the truth, and that might include confrontation, hearing a no, corrective feedback, or some information you haven't considered. The dreaded discussion!

If you're experiencing a conflict of expectations, find out what specifically is wanted and needed. What are people's interests that are not being served? How can they be served? What is the expectation that is not being met? What are your commitments and the commitments of others regarding the expectation? If it's important, make a commitment and get it done. If not, clear the air and move on.

**Turn any expectations into requests! If not, your
expectations will become complaints.**

Have you ever had a conflict of expectations and finally
you asked and the response you heard was, "Wow, why didn't
you ask sooner?" When you make a request you get a response.
Then you have the opportunity to get what you want, get new
information, negotiate an outcome, or get turned down. The
value of a "no" is to end the expectation that something is going
to happen with that particular person regarding your specific
request.

One of the most common conflicts of expectations is
around time. To ask others to get something done without giving
them a timeline is an expectation and it's easy to fix. There's
no commitment without a time frame. Train yourself to always
get the timeline clear when saying yes to any project and when
making a request of another person.

There's some soul searching you can do around
expectations in your relationships. Notice where you get
annoyed, aggravated, or irritated. It can reveal a growing
conflict of expectations. I've had people tell me about experiences
they've had in relationship seminars where one of the processes
is to make a list of all the qualities they want in another person.
When I ask them whether they bring those same qualities to
their relationships, they laugh and unabashedly say no. They
have expectations! What if you trade any idealized expectations
about relationships into a real relationship by giving voice to
your expectations? You may be surprised by the discovery of
who you are for another person and who they can be for you.

Conflict Of Values

If you're experiencing a conflict of values, examine your expressed or implied agreement to individual or organizational vision, values, purpose, and/or operating principles.

For example, if you value time with your family and your organization values 80-hour workweeks, you'll be in conflict either with your company or your family. A conflict of values is often more challenging to resolve and requires understanding clearly what people, family, and business value as a way of operating in the world. It may be that some businesses will say they value life balance, but in their day-to-day practices they operate differently.

I don't think there's a person in business today that hasn't heard of win-win solutions as a way to resolve conflict. I've heard from many managers and CEOs that win-win is a nice theory and they wish it could work but it doesn't. Why? Because they usually have win-win confused with giving in. Why does someone give in? They give in because they're tired of the conflict and want to get back to "normal", or they think they'll win the approval of the other person and they can use that for the future. They don't realize they can hang on to the resolution process until a solution is forged where both parties' interests are served. So, they give up, walk away defeated, or feel resentful or weak. This is especially true in a conflict of values. The practice is to continue to negotiate until a resolution is found.

Win-win can sound like both parties get what they want. That's not entirely accurate. Win-win is where both parties agree to a solution that serves their interests and may be different from their original positions. It's not win-win if you don't gain from the solution. Yet, most likely both parties have to give up something to discover a win-win. You have to stay committed to resolution until an outcome is discovered and all parties' interests are served.

In resolving a conflict of values, the results may not always be equal. The mistake that most people make in finding a solution to a conflict of values is a tendency to divide up a fixed pie, which ultimately may not be the best solution. A conflict of values can be the beginning of a true exploration of your vision of a life worth living. Values are clarified by asking yourself and others what matters most.

A Resolution

The following is an illustration: I was asked to coach a business owner who had an ongoing conflict with his partner that had escalated out of control, and was impacting the performance of everyone in their company. The request for coaching was indicative of his commitment to resolution.

**The first thing we did was separate the
problem from the conflict.**

The problem was how to expand the company. The conflict was about the different styles and values of the two partners. The solution was rather obvious and not hard to design or get the buy-in from all parties; the hard part was to keep them communicating non-defensively, especially when their emotions ran high. I was coaching one of the partners and we made a pact—he could get angry, criticize, and complain but only to me. When he participated in the conversations to resolve the conflict, he was a model of non-defensive listening. He didn't react and he kept his focus on solving the problem rather than escalating the conflict. He knew that getting angry would focus the energy of the negotiation on who was right and who was wrong, causing a rehashing of the past and keeping the focus off of the problem to be solved. He decided that a lean negotiation was better than staying in a partnership with someone who had a different vision of the company than he did. Now here's what happened. They divided up the company in an interesting way.

The partner I coached took a larger territory with fewer existing assets and formed a new company with very little capital, but a huge potential for development. It was hard to put a value on the larger territory, but it served that partner's interest, it served his vision of the future, and he was willing to take the risk that he could develop the territory. The other partner took a smaller territory that included most of the existing assets and kept the old company. They chose their territories based on what served their interests. One was comfortable with risk and the other partner was not—that was part of the conflict. Now, there were no bad people here; they just had different visions of the future and different goals for the company.

The partner I was coaching sold his newly formed company for millions three years later. The other partner still had his company ten years later; he was minding the store. Now who was right and who was wrong? Neither. They had different values. One valued adventure and risk, the other security. And one still had security and the other was on to the next adventure. We were able to resolve the conflict in a way that served them both. Interestingly enough, the one still running his stores called his old partner years later and asked him to help sell the remaining company. They had a great conversation about what each of them had learned over their years apart and agreed to work together on the sale. It was sold for a great profit. Lesson learned? Not only was the conflict resolved, the relationship lasted over time with a respect for what each person brought to the enterprise.

Unfortunately in many conflicts people don't understand that their values, styles, or expectations are clashing. So they make the decision that they're right and the other person or group of people is not only wrong, they're jerks. This kind of thinking doesn't lead to anything but a deeper entrenchment of a position.

The first thing you want two people, two groups, or two nations to focus on to resolve conflict is a commitment to resolution. You must have a commitment to resolution in order to get people to the "table" and discover a solution that will work over time.

Think about when you want to improve your performance or fulfill a goal. You must first generate the belief that it is possible to improve; that it's possible for you to achieve an intended goal. In conflict situations you must generate the belief that it's possible to resolve the conflict.

Step Into Someone Else's Shoes

How do you know when you're committed to resolution rather than committed to being right? You'll know it because you'll be willing to step off your position and even step into the other person's shoes. Why? So you can appreciate the full implications of their position, opinion, interests, intention, and point of view. You're willing to stay in the process long enough for discovery to take place and inform new solutions. A

145

commitment to resolution lasts through the implementation of the solution, including the breakdowns that might occur with an intention to tweak the plan as necessary.

To loosen your hold on your position, especially a deeply held point of view, and move to a commitment for resolution before you know the plan to resolve the issue, is not an easy task. It's hard to do. Having said that, if it were not a deeply held conviction you would have resolved the issue already.

Practice A Commitment To Resolution

A commitment to resolution allows you to open up to consider another perspective, and provides a very important practice in resolving conflict. This practice gives you the room to know as much as possible about the person or group with whom you're having the conflict. Stepping into someone's shoes allows you to get a glimpse of the world from their eyes. This gives you valuable information. It says you are committed to finding a way to resolve the conflict and solve the problems, even though right now you don't know what the solution is going to look like.

Sometimes you may need to declare a "cooling off period" to get some coaching or just step away to get some perspective. However without a resulting commitment to resolution you won't move on to discuss solutions authentically that will solve the problem and start building a relationship of trust.

A commitment to resolution doesn't mean people have to like each other. It transcends likes/dislikes.

A commitment to resolution says that you are more committed to finding solutions than to being right; more committed to healing than to violence; more committed to connection than to separation; more committed to what's possible now than to holding on to past grievances.

Once you're committed to resolution you can ask questions and identify what people want and need, and why. You can determine the nature of the problem or breakdown. You can learn from what you've already done and discover corrections. You're actually beginning the creation process in the cycle of fulfillment. Many ideas can be formulated and discussed before you ever get to the point of deciding and agreeing on a solution. A commitment to resolution says you will defeat the problem not each other. Then you can gain clarity about differences in styles, expectations, and values that may be at the core of the conflict.

Practice: *Identify any conflict you are currently engaged in and separate the problem from the conflict. What is the problem that needs to be solved? Identify the type of conflict. Is it a conflict of styles, values or expectations? The practice here is to just notice what escalates conflict and what resolves conflict. The resolution process is outlined in Chapter 17.*

It seems to me that conflict doesn't get integrated until you learn the lessons that the conflict can teach you. Identify any limiting stories you tell about the people involved or the situation itself. Why is this important? When you have limiting stories, you don't move into a cycle of fulfillment; instead you continue to fuel a cycle of disappointment. The fulfillment in conflict is learning, waking up, and creating a breakthrough. Learning to deal with conflict effectively is essential to being aware and it's essential to a life worth living.

Chapter 16

Finding The Third Possibility

"You never change things by fighting the existing reality. To change something, build a new model that makes the existing model obsolete."
R. *Buckminster Fuller*

Let me give you an example of how you can address a conflict when it's occurring. I'll use a business example and change the names to protect the innocent. Mike comes into my office and says, "I just can't get along with George. I can't work with him on this project. George is impossible to work with and not only do I think George is impossible to work with, everyone thinks George is impossible to work with."

Let's take this step by step. Mike has a complaint about George. Remember conflicts of expectation come out of unresolved complaints. If Mike has a complaint about George, you want to identify the problem and the source of the complaint. What specifically? You don't have to agree or disagree about the nature of the complaint. Don't try to talk someone out of it or gloss over it. Instead you acknowledge what someone is saying.

In the case of Mike and George, it went something like this: "Thanks, Mike, for coming in. Let's talk about this. It sounds like you want to get this resolved. What's actually happening that would cause you to say that you can't work with George?" When you ask questions you will be able to find out what happened and be able to disentangle the problem from the apparent conflict of expectations. Then you can help Mike generate for himself an authentic commitment to resolution.

When there is a conflict, whether at home or at work, it is imperative to separate the people from the problem. Where there is conflict there are usually some stylistic differences between the people involved that get magnified in the dispute. Let's take this example a little bit further:

When I asked Mike what actually happened, he said, "I can't work with him because all he does is get on my back or my people when a mistake is made, even when we're already on track to correct it. And he never acknowledges my team when we accomplish the goal." Sound familiar?

Let's see what we can learn from this conflict with Mike and George. Mike doesn't think he can influence George. I wanted to leave Mike with a commitment to resolution and in action to solve the problem and resolve the conflict. The opportunity was to help Mike move off his position so he could see the conflict differently.

Forced Choice

What do you do when somebody has already made a decision or come to the conclusion that nothing will work, short of replacing George? You can't help the situation if you think that Mike is right and that George is impossible to work with. You don't want to be trapped in a forced choice, to agree or disagree, to fire George or have Mike quit; you want to be open to a third possibility.

I read an interview that Bill Moyers had with Michael Josephson who, when I met him, headed an organization called

Josephson Bar Review for Lawyers. He was discussing ethics with Bill Moyers and spoke clearly about his progress in coming to terms with ethical choices that transcend the exclusive needs of one group versus another, and taking into consideration all possibilities. I was left with the thought that until people have a third possibility they don't really have an ethical choice. As I considered this I realized that without a third possibility what you have is an either/or scenario ... a forced choice.

We're conditioned to think that there is only "our way" or "my way" choices. When you think this way, regardless of the outcome, someone is going to feel like or think they got the short end of the stick. If you have a role in resolving conflict, it's to find the third possibility. The third possibility opens up a conversation to solve the problem and resolve the conflict. The third possibility allows you to let go of attachment to a specific outcome and be free to consider the best outcome for all concerned.

Think about the two cycles discussed earlier. One is a cycle of fulfillment and the other is a cycle of disappointment. Notice the statement that "George is impossible to work with." What cycle is that in? It's a limiting story in the cycle of disappointment and prevents any action that doesn't agree with that story. It doesn't mean that Mike had no evidence to support his story; he did have evidence. We are great at collecting evidence to support our "rightness" about any conflict. Our attachment to being right however doesn't lead to resolution.

Attachment gets in the way of discovering any ideas that will resolve the situation (outside of your way) and end the complaint.

Why do we collect evidence, hold on to limiting stories,

and continue to be attached to being right knowing that it fuels the conflict? I was giving a presentation at a conference and there were several hundred people in the audience. I was talking about these ideas and spoke about the limiting stories that people have about each other that can actually hold the conflict in place. During the question-and-answer period a woman got very agitated as she said, "Now wait a minute. You're telling me that what I say about my boss is a limiting story? Well then you don't know my boss!"

After the laughter died down I asked her to tell me her "story" about her boss. She said, "Well, she is loud and angry. She interrupts people and she's always right and does exactly what she wants to do regardless of what other people say. She'll ask for input when she's already made decisions and then doesn't change her mind." Now this lady continued with her story until she wound down and then asked me, "Now does that sound like a story?" I responded by asking, "Is what you say about your boss impacting your results?" She said, "Yes. I'm constantly aggravated and upset. I resist what she says and she knows it, which doesn't help me with my performance reviews." And then I asked her, "Well, what are you going to do about that?" And she said, "Well, I can't change her. There's nothing I can do." She was halfway there. It was true that she couldn't change her boss. What I asked her to do was to question whether her statement "there was nothing she could do" was the truth, or a limiting story based on her past behavior.

How many times have we decided there was nothing that could be done but we still tell the story and continue to collect evidence to prove that we are right? So what we're saying in effect is, "I'm a victim of circumstances. I'm a victim of the way people operate." And then we stop looking for alternatives.

We often use other people's behavior as a reason not to intervene, not to tell the truth, not to give feedback, or not even to disagree. We use it as a reason to give up. When we operate this way we are saying that we are powerless in the face of the condition or the person. Instead ... consider there is something that can be done.

The Third Possibility In Action

During this presentation I facilitated a process where people could sit with another participant as their coach. They were given the task of taking one of their toughest conflict stories and not only coming up with possible solutions, but also committing to implementing them in the following 72 hours. I also asked them to stay in touch with their coach and report on what happened.

The same woman who shared her story about the conflict with her boss came up to me at the end and said, "I can't believe I was able to come up with any ideas for a solution. I realized I'd put myself in an either/or position—either they transfer her or I'm leaving. Coming up with a third and even fourth and fifth possibility was so freeing. I started to think about what I would want someone to do if I were acting inappropriately in a meeting. Would I want them to talk to other people about me? No. I would want them to come to me."

It was a similar situation with Mike and George. I had the following conversation with Mike: "Okay, let's just say George is not the problem. Then what would you say is the problem?" Mike said, "Well, I'm not getting the acknowledgment I deserve." Then I asked, "What could you do to get the acknowledgment?" Mike said, "I don't know, you'll have to talk to George." I chuckled and said, "I'm not talking to George; I'm talking to you. George didn't ask me for help, you did! What could you do?"

Remember until someone owns the problem and the conflict as theirs they can't solve the problem or resolve the conflict. Taking 100% accountability is actually very freeing. It's the source of personal power to shape your response to what is happening.

100% accountability allows you to recover from reaction and step up to who you are.

You realize that you are creating, promoting, or allowing your response to what is happening now and what can take place now. When you acknowledge that this is your problem you can begin to come up with solutions. You also realize if you do nothing, you're allowing what you don't want to continue. People recognize when someone is operating from 100% accountability. It demonstrates personal power. It inspires confidence.

Mike had to own the conflict. In conflict situations it's very easy to blame the other person for something that you're not getting, rather than taking the action to resolve the issue. Often when there is a conflict of expectations and you're not getting something you expect or think is fair, the other person may not even be aware that a conflict exists. Think about the times you suffered over giving critical feedback and then you gave it and the response created an opening for ongoing feedback. Your distress about unresolved conflict can end sooner if you address it when it happens.

Another question I asked Mike is "Have you asked George for feedback or directly asked him 'Well what do you think of the results we got on this project? How'd we do? Give me your assessment.'" Mike said, "Well, no, I didn't ask. Why should I have to ask? Isn't acknowledging people one of the basic assumptions of effective management?" Yes it is. And you ask for what you want and need because the power for action is in your hands. Fulfillment is in the action you take right now. Stop waiting.

This is as true in your own relationships as it is with Mike and George. It's OK to ask and it's fine to remind your spouse to remember your anniversary or some other important date. Let go of the common story that if you have to remind her it takes all the fun out of it. That's not a recipe for fulfillment.

Turn Your Complaints Into Requests

When you realize a complaint is at the core of any conflict and you're committed to resolution, consciously stop complaining and turn your complaints into requests. Start negotiating a resolution that benefits all concerned and don't stop until the conflict ends. A successful resolution only ends lingering complaints if you stop complaining and develop the ability to ask for what you want. A request initiates action— ultimately a yes or a no. A request is a powerful way for you to be in action to accomplish your goals, now and in the future. It's also a powerful way for you to influence people.

When you make a request for feedback or give feedback, it's important that it's real and about results. Inauthentic praise is seen as a "got to do" or a "management theory" and is not effective. Authentic praise is felt and heard. Authentic feedback allows you to correct your course of action and learn from mistakes.

Now let's return to our scenario with Mike and George one final time. Mike asked for the feedback. He made the request of George to acknowledge his team and he added that it would mean a lot to him and his team to hear it directly from George. The answer was yes. They scheduled a time to make it happen. And George admitted something to Mike. He said he knew that he didn't take the time to acknowledge people. It was something he was working on, and he asked Mike to coach him if it was missing again. When Mike turned his complaint into a request he initiated a conversation for resolution. He turned the conflicts of expectations and style into a new model ... a model of direct communication that could be responded to with dialogue, possibilities, and real commitment, plus he gained the ability to communicate with his boss.

Practice: *Notice any forced choices today. They're easily identified as times when it appears there are only two unfavorable options, an either/or scenario. Ask what else is possible and you will engage the third possibility practice.*

Turn your complaints into requests or into a promise to take action. Make requests and take action that brings an end to any limiting stories, resolves the conflict, and solves the problem.

Remember, you're not requesting that someone stop being a jerk or a (you fill in the blank)! That they're a "blank" is your story. Instead you're requesting what you want and need. This is a simple practice that starts with an inquiry to reveal what is wanted and needed. Start today with small annoyances and you'll build a practice that works for a lifetime.

Chapter 17

Five Steps To Resolution

"I first learned the concepts of non-violence in my marriage." Mahatma
Gandhi

Whether the conflict is styles, expectations, or values,
consider using the following five steps the next time
you find yourself in conflict. These five steps will allow you to
operate in the cycle of fulfillment and resolve conflict or difficult
situations at home or on the job. It will be helpful to remember
these steps, especially if you get in the middle of a conflict and
it's not going anywhere.

The First Step Is Discovery

Discovery happens in the creation phase in the cycle of
fulfillment when you commit to resolution, before you know how
to resolve the conflict or what specifically the solution will be.
Discovery begins when you generate agreement that resolution
is possible.

Ask yourself and the people involved to set aside any
limiting stories or prejudicial statements about the participants.
Ask questions to find out the conclusions participants have
already come to, and help them loosen their grip on those
conclusions. This is where you get to practice letting go of
attachment to any one point of view so you can listen, and ask
questions. You do this so everyone involved can get clear about

the stories they tell that limit a resolution and their ability to solve a problem. You lead the way by letting go of attachment so you help others commit to resolution. You don't bring people you are in conflict with to the table by calling them stupid or evil. And yet habitually, we'll tell others and ourselves limiting stories about the people and companies we deal with, instead of solving the problems that are at the core of the conflicts in which we find ourselves. We need to break that habit.

When you commit to resolution you take your focus off the complaint or limiting story and put it where it needs to be ... on the problem to be solved. You separate the problem from the conflict. You find out whether it's a conflict of styles, expectations, or values and help clarify for yourself and others how to be with differences in styles and values, and how to turn an expectation into a request or possible solution. Then you and others can invent and entertain new possibilities. You can actually begin to engage more fully in the possibility that the conflict and the problem will be resolved.

Through dialogue and discussion, options and alternatives will be discovered that could serve the interests of the individual and the organization, two colleagues, two departments, partners or family members. Forcing a solution before you know the interests and requests of all parties may not net you the best outcome.

Remember a commitment to resolution is number one. When you are focused on resolution you can separate the stories about what happened from the facts of what happened. You learn more about the conflict of styles, expectations, and values. You discover the facts on which everyone can agree.

You don't leave this step of discovery until you get a commitment to resolution from everyone involved, you've uncovered and agreed on the problem to solve, and you've been able to sort through and invent as many possible solutions as you can. The last step in the discovery process is to focus and agree on the possibility that is workable and that all parties are committed to, because it solves the problem and serves the interests of all concerned.

The Second Step Is Design

Design happens in the phase of manifestation in the cycle of fulfillment because you are now asking the questions that tell you how you are going to implement this solution, and by when. In the design part of the resolution process you sit down and plan a successful strategy to implement the solution.

In the first phase you discovered and agreed on what to do; now you need to agree on how. Guard against a pullback to the conflict. Continue to ask questions like: "How would that work?" or "Let's think about the results of that action. What would be the impact?" You stay in the design conversation until a clear course of action emerges.

You determine whether there are any other people whose agreement you need to ensure a successful implementation. You're clear about what the agreements are, and who does what. You're clear and in agreement on dates by when things will happen. You put it in writing. You have everyone sign off on the solution and design the structure for fulfillment.

You also design a procedure in case of future breakdowns. This can take the form of a regular meeting or a scheduled communication to report on what happened—a scorecard that reports on progress. This is prevention. It's done to prevent future conflict and it is a call for action if progress is halted. Progress is not automatic; it needs to be followed and tracked.

Think about preventive measures you can build into the design now. What are some early warning signs you can recognize and deal with sooner rather than later? You might want to identify and build in to the resolution process a designated coach. If anyone gets stuck they can ask for coaching.

Now, with an agreed-upon design in hand you move into the third step. You are still operating in the manifestation phase of the cycle of fulfillment.

The Third Step Is Action

Just talking about what you will do is never enough. It may bring relief but it will not sustain resolution over time until you take action to implement the designed plan and keep your new agreements. Carefully consider the agreements you make in the design phase so you're left with an unswerving intention to fulfill what you say you will do.

Following these three steps—discovery, design, and action—has considerable potential for building a new relationship based on mutual commitments, and the experience of having successfully worked together to resolve conflict and solve problems.

You are now speaking about the conflict and any person you had a "story" about differently because you and the others are in action. Let me repeat this. It's important. I've noticed some people continue with their old complaining story out of habit, even after the conflict and problem have been solved. If someone you work with repeats one of your old stories about the other person back to you or to others, clear it up by saying, "You know we worked on that together and got it resolved." The other person might respond, "Well, really, you were so upset, what happened?" Use it as an opportunity to talk about the process and what you learned. You will inspire people through your words, thoughts, and actions and end the use of limiting stories as a replacement for well-planned action. You will be part of creating a culture of fulfillment versus a culture of blame.

The Fourth Step Is Feedback

Feedback tells you whether the solution worked or didn't work. If it did work, you can move to the fifth step. If it didn't work, you go back to the first step of discovery and move through the process again empowered by what you've learned so far. You maintain your commitment to resolution and design a plan that works. Once a commitment to resolution is firmly in place people find solutions that are effective, even if they have to revisit the discovery process and begin again. Step 1—discovery—happens in the creation phase of the cycle of fulfillment. Steps 2 through 4 happen in the manifestation phase of the cycle of fulfillment—because you're still working on manifesting the result.

What follows is an example of the importance of staying committed to a resolution. I worked with two people who had equal power in an organization and a deeply entrenched conflict that went back many years. There was a clear problem to be solved. In fact, there were proposals and counterproposals to solve the problem. But what continued to get in the way was the conflict between these two people and their inability to separate each other from the problem. So the focus continually moved off of solving the problem to getting back at each other. It took on biblical proportions of an eye for an eye.

All three conflicts—styles, expectations, and values— were in place here. There was a conflict of styles. One person was very relationship-oriented. He had surrendered his position in the past and then resented it, and could not understand why this other person was so controlling and mean-spirited. Consequently he dug in his heels. The other person was very results-oriented. He wouldn't give up any control and came across as unrelenting. He couldn't understand why his counterpart was so capricious, emotional, and disrespectful.

They also had a conflict of expectations. One partner thought he had an agreement on a project and the other insisted no agreement was made, even though the company had already invested a considerable sum of money in the project. He said it didn't constitute an agreement, only an exploration to see whether they were going to continue. And then there was a conflict of values. One wanted to use profits to develop and invest in new projects. The other wanted to use profits to repay debt. One valued risk and expansion, the other security and stewardship.

It became increasingly difficult to solve the problem as the focus stayed on the stories about how wrong the other person was, and the feeling escalated on both sides that no solution was possible short of dividing up everything. That solution sounds simple but took years and lawyers and a deepening division in the organization.

When people don't acknowledge what the core of the conflict is really about and instead continue to attack each other, the result is disappointment and blame rather than fulfillment built on a foundation of accountability. Whether in our organizations or in our families, we can easily lose sight of what we can accomplish if we resolve the conflict and solve the problem. In this situation, there was a tremendous cost to each person's sense of fulfillment, and to their families, and their own peace of mind. They eventually solved the problem but the conflict was not resolved and led to an enduring separation.

I'm interested in freeing people from their limiting stories. So I continue to look at why people seem to persist with their limiting stories, even when they recognize there's a difference in styles, expectations, or values. What causes someone to stay stuck and attached to their position? Why is their need to be right so high? What prevents them from letting go, if even for a moment, so they could consider something new? When I've asked these kinds of questions people tell me they don't think they're wrong. They don't say, "I have a story about my partner but maybe I'm wrong about it!" They say, "I have a story about my partner and I'm right!" They may recognize their story limits their range of action, but they still believe they're right.

The challenge is to let go of your attachment to being right and replace it with awareness and attention. Your attachment to being right actually prevents you from seeing anything you don't already believe, and what you already believe is blocking your progress. That's when it's beneficial to have a resolution process that includes letting go of attachment.

This fourth step—feedback—is critical to the conflict resolution process. If you revert to a limiting story like "I knew it wouldn't work!" instead of going forward to discover what you learned, what's missing, and how to refine the process, you're doomed to deepen the conflict. Don't use feedback to derail your commitment to resolution. Get back on course quickly, find out what happened, and look at what's possible now.

Once the feedback tells you the solution worked you can move to the fifth step.

The Fifth Step Is Completion

At this point it's important to declare to everyone involved that the conflict is complete and the problem is solved.

Acknowledge the people who made it possible. Review the process and what you learned. Celebrate your success and resolve to use this process again when conflict occurs. The five-step process outlined here will help you resolve conflict, no matter how big or small, so you can be fulfilled both on the journey to resolution and with the result. The further work is to wake up and realize what got in the way of fulfillment in the first place, and use these steps to prevent conflict from escalating out of control.

At the end of the resolution process ask each individual whether they are complete and to articulate their commitment should a conflict arise in the future. When each person says, "I'm complete and should any conflict arise in the future I am committed to bringing it up and resolving it when it first arises!" you'll know that you've been successful using this five-step resolution process.

Practice: *Identify any current conflict or disagreement and use this five-step process to resolve the issues.*

1. *Discovery*
2. *Design*
3. *Action*
4. *Feedback*
5. *Completion*

Then notice what happens to your fulfillment.

Chapter 18

Commitment: Yes Or No!

"The self is not something ready-made, but something in continuous formation through choice of action." John Dewey

It's important to remember when you make requests that you may not always get a yes response. When someone says no, that's a commitment, even though you may want him to say yes. He's not saying no to you, he's saying no to your request. I believe in the power of that two-letter word. If it's no, I want to know it.

Making requests and asking questions are integral to relationships, resolving conflict, and getting things done. Questions are requests for information. Why don't we make more requests or ask more questions? Well, one reason is it throws you into the unknown. You don't know whether you're going to get a yes or a no response. When you ask people questions you may hear things you didn't anticipate. If you can listen to what someone says non-defensively and without attachment, you can take the information and learn something new.

Sometimes you may not ask because you assume you know! In an earlier chapter, I wrote about asking for someone to tell you the truth. In order for someone to tell you the truth, you have to be able to listen and entertain it. I'm reminded of the Jack Nicholson line in *A Few Good Men* when he stated, "You can't handle the truth!"

Aristotle said it best: "It is the mark of an educated mind to be able to entertain a thought without accepting it." I would humbly add to that statement: it is the mark of an educated mind to be able to make a request without any fear of hearing no. Concern about hearing no can prevent you from making your request to the appropriate person. Ask and you might be surprised.

Sometimes people may not want to ask because they think putting others on the spot to say yes or no makes them uncomfortable. If you think yes is the only possible response to a request, you may even find yourself avoiding people you think make requests that put you on the spot. Requests do put you on the spot. They put you on the spot to say yes or no.

It seems that people who utilize the avoidance philosophy prefer to grumble or just talk with other people who really can't make a difference relative to their request or concern. This philosophy can quickly turn into being perceived as someone who complains or even has good ideas but doesn't take action on those ideas. When you delve into this approach you realize there's little, if any, fulfillment in not making requests when they're required for you to get things done, resolve conflict, or fulfill your vision of a life worth living.

If avoidance of making requests or listening to requests feels familiar, practice making requests and just listen to the person's response. And practice listening to any request without fear that you'll be coerced into a yes. You can say no with a smile instead of giving all the reasons why you can't say yes. You can listen to a request and entertain it without saying yes.

At some point you may begin to realize agreement is not automatic. However, if you don't ask, the answer is automatically no. Coach yourself and others to make the request, and then let the other person or group of people respond. Then listen. You can begin with a clarifying question so you can get some information before you make a request. Coach yourself and others not to decide in advance what someone is going to say. This is an essential fulfillment practice. Don't answer for them. This becomes easier when you're not attached to the outcome. This is a time when the "high participation, low attachment" practice comes in handy! You continue to participate and be committed to what you want to achieve. You let go of attachment to a person saying yes without giving up on your goal. With this practice you have an important realization for yourself and others.

No is what makes choice possible.

When you're going to make a request, think in advance what questions someone might ask. Be prepared so you can answer questions thoroughly. Do your homework. When you ask a question, you get information.

When you make a request, you get commitment. So if the commitment is a yes, you're clear on what, who, when, how, and where. And if the response is no, you're clear it's a no to what you're requesting. A "no" response may tell you that you need to do more homework or rethink your request.

If you listen to no as a rejection, it's hard for you to hear it as an opening. What can no be an opening for? It can be the opening to ask someone else. It can give you the opportunity to learn someone isn't interested in what you're interested in or they're committed to something else. It can give you the opportunity to understand that no can be listened to as the beginning of a negotiation. You can explore other possibilities.

Have you ever wanted to say yes to a request but you said no? Why does that happen? Because you may already be committed to something else, and saying yes will put your current commitments in jeopardy; you could end up with broken agreements. You don't want broken agreements because you know they can cause or escalate conflict. So, you say no even when it's hard to do.

When you understand the power of yes and no, you appreciate what it means to have an agreement. It means you have an explicit promise that a specific action will take place in a specific time frame. Agreements are different from having an unmet expectation. Conflicts of expectation happen because there isn't clarity upfront on what, who, how, where, and—most importantly—by when. An expectation in the cycle of disappointment is where you have a fantasy based on an assumption that something's going to be done or someone will take action. Those are expectations inside of fantasy that are missing true commitment and authentic communication.

Your fulfillment exits quickly when you say yes and don't mean it. It also exits quickly when you accept someone's yes and you know it's questionable. You'll know you're concerned when you talk to yourself about why you said yes or why you didn't speak up when you had doubts about someone else's agreement.

As soon as you know that you don't have complete agreement, go back and deal with it. You may have to rescind your "yes." You may have to ask clarifying questions of the person who gave you a half-hearted yes and ask, "Does this work for you?" and then listen. It's in your interest not to be caught by surprise later on when a promise isn't fulfilled.

I've taught my staff this idea. If they think they don't have full agreement from me, they'll pop back in my office or call me and say, "Paulette, I didn't get a time frame from you. When can you have that information for me?" or "Does this work for you?" And then we schedule it, map it out, and get the resources we need to complete the promise or get someone else involved who can move the project forward.

A commitment says we're not leaving anything to chance and we'll deal with the truly unexpected along the way.

Practice: *Listen carefully to the requests that are made of you today. Say no to what you don't want to do or can't fulfill given your current commitments.*

Listen to requests without concern for what people will think if you say no. Say no without remorse or impatience.

If you have any promises you've said yes to and haven't completed, examine them closely, and if you know you're not going to fulfill them, tell the truth to yourself and any others who are involved in the promise so you can revoke your promise or renegotiate.

Chapter 19

Broken Agreements

"We must not promise what we ought not, lest we be called on to perform what we cannot." Abraham Lincoln

Here's the first paradox about agreements:

Keep all the promises you make and recognize that broken agreements will happen.

My business and fulfillment philosophy is to just do it right the first time so you don't have to fix it later. However, life teaches me that breakdowns happen even with the best-laid plans. It's not that broken agreements or problems happen; it's what you do next that makes a difference or knocks you off the path both to being fulfilled and achieving your goals.

When someone breaks an agreement with you, what do you notice? The first thing people usually say is, "Broken agreements diminish trust. I don't know whether I can count on that person again." You may also notice that if the broken agreement remains unaddressed you can actually feel it; there's something between you and the other person. It's important to deal with broken agreements immediately. Remember this fulfillment practice: confront problems, conflicts, and broken agreements when they first arise.

Did We Have An Agreement?

The first question to ask someone if there's a broken agreement is "Did we have an agreement?" Check it out. You may be surprised to learn that sometimes where you thought there was an agreement there may not have been a clear time frame. When you are clear about the promises you make, your agreements will be unambiguous and include time frames and what it will take to fulfill the agreement. However, it's still interesting to ask, "Did we have an agreement?" because sometimes you'll find out that you thought there was agreement, but there was no ownership on the part of the other person. They said yes because they felt they had to. And the first indication to you that they didn't mean it was when they broke their agreement.

**Acknowledge broken agreements,
renegotiate, and end your suffering.**

It's important to create environments where people can say yes and no freely at home and at work. If your family and business associates know you are going to hold them to their word and they also hold you to your word, you will all carefully consider commitments and make authentic agreements.

It's sometimes startling to realize that if you are accepting promises from a person who continues to break their agreements with you, you are as accountable as the other person. Why is that? Because you are operating in a cycle of disappointment with a fantasy that it's going to be different next time. Perhaps you have a limiting story that you have to be the nice guy. You can ask, "What's going to be different next time?" Then you can consider and state the consequence if it's not different. The consequence becomes part of the promise.

I don't know about you, but it still aggravates me when I give a deadline to please someone else—whether a customer, colleague, or family member—that I know when I'm saying it that it's doubtful, or it will put pressure on me to perform. You can break yourself of that habit, or at least put a dent in it, by giving yourself time to think over a commitment before you make it. Whether five minutes or overnight, the notion of "sleeping on it" is an effective fulfillment practice. You may think of further questions to ask, especially if you're taking on a big promise in the world that involves several people or departments. Allow yourself time to reflect on whether or not you can deliver if you say yes.

I find the power in this is twofold: I only make commitments I intend to keep and I give people time to think things over before making a commitment to me. I've said it before and it's good to remind you here that agreement is not automatic. If you think you will regret your decision or you often wonder why you didn't say no or ask more questions upfront, it's an indication to slow down and carefully consider what you're saying yes to and why you're saying yes. In the practice of fulfillment, you want to have the opportunity to consider the choice you're making before you make it.

What Happened?

If you ask, "Did we have an agreement?" and the answer is "Yes," what is the next question you might ask? The question I ask is "What happened?" You ask this question to give you information that will assist you in resolving the breakdown.

What often occurs around a broken agreement is someone waits and waits until they get angry or frustrated, building a limiting story about the other person until they finally say something out of anger before they get any information. Impatience and anger usually occur because you wait to confront the broken agreement, or it has happened over and over and you continue to accept someone's promise without any difference in the outcome.

Remember the old saying—insanity is doing the same thing over and over expecting different results. This is a great definition of fantasy in the cycle of disappointment. Instead of continuing the fantasy ask clarifying questions like "Did we have an agreement?" and "What happened?" After careful discussion, it becomes clear whether a person, vendor, or co-worker can fulfill the promise or not and whether they can negotiate a new commitment and keep it. If not, you can move on.

When you make effective agreements you find out in advance whether someone is capable of fulfilling their promise. This mindful process helps you and it helps them. Hold people accountable with compassion. When you keep the promises you make and help others keep theirs, you will deliver on the promise of fulfillment.

Renegotiate

In business and in life you sometimes make agreements and then realize at some point that you're not going to be able to follow through. As soon as you know don't put off talking to the people involved. Get online with the person you made the promise to and renegotiate. Work with them to understand what happened (just the facts, please) and make a new agreement. For the most part people will understand. They don't like surprises. They don't want to know at the last minute or when it's due. They want to know and sign off on any new plan of action. They want to know as soon as you know. However, if you continually renegotiate your agreements that's a signal to spend more time upfront deliberating on whether or not the time frame is accurate, or that you can actually fulfill the agreements you or your organization are making.

One of the great stressors in life is not keeping your agreements. It diminishes trust and causes conflict with others; it also diminishes self-trust and causes internal conflict on whether you can be successful. It intrudes on your fulfillment.

Think about the times you made a simple promise to be on time. What do you notice you do if you realize you're going to be late? Do you rehearse stories? "It was the traffic," "It was that phone call, I had to take it," "It was that report, I had to finish it." We tend to blame our broken agreements on conditions. But when you face the broken agreement without the story, the answer to the question "What happened?" is different. The answer on reflection is often a variation on the following: "Instead of leaving on time so I could arrive on time, I did one more phone call, one more load of wash, one more email … all inside of my control."

With that understanding, you begin to notice what you make more important than keeping your promises and achieving your intended results. And you notice what you make more important than being on time. This kind of self-inquiry helps you think about your promises, so you can make your choices with awareness.

When you operate in a cycle of disappointment you end up with a limiting story that usually has blame in it, or places you in the position of being a victim of circumstances. "Well, my boss came in and asked me to do a quick report, I had to do it. Nothing I could do about it. You know how she is." When you face yourself in a cycle of fulfillment you have the opportunity to learn from broken agreements, so you can break the pattern or respond differently. Have you ever considered that you can tell your boss in the morning that you have to leave by a certain time so any last-minute requests will be done the next day? It is possible, it just takes some thoughtful planning.

What happens after someone has made an agreement with you and they revoke their promise? The truth is you can revoke a promise. However, there are consequences to revoking promises. Trust can be diminished. There also can be legal/financial consequences if a contract was signed, which is why contracts are written, to clarify and obtain clear promises. If you notice that you habitually break agreements, or others break their agreements with you, I encourage you to carefully consider the promises you make ... and receive.

Hold Others Accountable

Empower the people you have agreements with by following up. Consider this example: I was consulting the board of directors and staff of a non-profit organization. The volunteer coordinator had a hard time holding people accountable for the promises they made. Her limiting story was "Well, this isn't a business. You can't hold volunteers accountable for their agreements." So I conducted a survey of volunteers. This is what they told me. When no one followed up on their broken agreements, they felt like it didn't really matter; that no one really cared. And here's the most interesting outcome—they stopped volunteering.

Not holding the volunteers accountable for keeping their promises also said to the other volunteers who kept their commitments that the organization didn't have a commitment to excellence. This was a major wake-up call for the volunteer coordinator. She started a new program with the volunteers. She asked for and got their commitment and held them accountable for what they said they would do. This new commitment to excellence quickly spread throughout the group. Volunteers realized that what they did was important and valued by the organization, and the number of volunteers grew from fifty to over three hundred within a year.

When I say hold people accountable with compassion, I mean that you don't need to get worked up, attack someone, make them wrong, or give in; just put the issue on the table so it can be discussed and resolved. It's essential to your development and it's essential to their development.

When you talk to people about their broken agreements, you end suffering—theirs and yours. You move the focus to completion and to achieving results. Declare a breakdown as soon as you know you are not going to keep an agreement and keep in mind this second paradox about agreements:

Keep all the agreements you make and recognize that if you're keeping all the agreements you make, your agreements may be too cautious. It may be time to make a bigger promise.

Practice: *If people have broken agreements with you, call them, hold them accountable. Ask, "Did we have an agreement?" and "What happened?" Clear it up by renegotiating the commitment and getting a clear "yes" or "no."*

If you have any current broken agreements, I encourage you to get them handled. Broken agreements hang around like distracting thoughts and sound like this: "I really need to do something about that" or "I've got to get to that." When you make the call, have the conversation, schedule the action, and do it, you move gratefully into fulfillment, and you're complete.

When you finish what's incomplete, you get back your focus and ability to concentrate on what's in front of you and what's important for you to achieve. Set up a daily practice of completion by noting what you need to do today to be complete, and keep your word with yourself and others.

Chapter 20

Fulfillment With Difficult People

"Love does not consist in gazing at each other, but in looking together in the same direction." Saint Exupéry

Who is difficult for you? What makes them difficult? Is there anyone who sees them differently? Usually when I ask people these questions, they tell me, "Well, my co-worker gets along with them." Why? What is the co-worker doing that works? Most likely they're not seeing that person as difficult. They are seeing that person as they are. That doesn't mean they don't notice the same things you do; it's just that they don't put a negative spin on what they see.

How you "see" another person is an interpretation.

You can see the same thing someone else sees; they just don't react to it. They may see someone as a bottom-line person. You may see the same person as someone who doesn't listen or doesn't care about people. The difference is it doesn't stop your co-worker from communicating with this "difficult" person. So they're able to move beyond what stops you and deal effectively in their interactions and communication. They don't walk away grumbling that the person doesn't care and doesn't listen, and they can probably ask clarifying questions that help them be more effective with that "difficult" person.

It could be that your co-worker is a bottom-line person as well, or has come to appreciate the differences. However, if we can't come to appreciate, or at least understand differences enough to solve problems, we tend to get more embroiled in conflicts of expectations, styles, and values. And then we'll often need mediators or lawyers to negotiate the differences.

It's essential in building relationships to gain some clarity on your underlying assumptions and rules and how they differ from others.

Assumptions And Rules

When we're talking to people they're operating, just like we are, from a set of paradigms. A paradigm is a pattern, a set of rules and regulations that define the world, as you know it. It's the "right" way to think, do, consider, plan, communicate, and act from your point of view or training. This includes how you've been conditioned by family, friends, school, experience, and culture to think, speak and act.

Your paradigm defines everything from how to make Thanksgiving dinner to how to talk to people. My husband's family is from the South and they have rules about being polite, and about what you can and can't say. They don't question the rules—it just "is" right.

It's hard to see or understand something outside of your paradigm. This idea is illustrated by the two well-known tests on the following page.

**Connect all 9 dots with 4 straight lines
without lifting your pen off the paper, or going
through any dot more than once.**

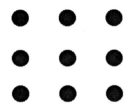

By adding just one line turn this diagram into a 6.

Often, people assume you have to stay inside the dots to solve the first puzzle. Once you see what you believe, you may stop looking or considering there might be a different or additional solution. It seems to be part of our human nature to make assumptions. The assumption in the IX process that many people make is you can only use a straight line to turn the diagram IX into the number 6. The challenge is not that we make assumptions—it's that we don't often question them. [See the last page of this chapter for solutions.]

If you're going to think outside the box, you have to suspend what you know "is" right and exchange it for what's possible. It's that simple, and at the same time, that complex because generally people aren't aware of their own paradigms or beliefs as a set of rules that govern their behavior and their ideas of what's right and wrong.

Think about temperature. There's Celsius and Fahrenheit. The Celsius paradigm says that freezing is at 0 degrees and boiling is at 100. That's a spread of 100. Fahrenheit says that freezing is at 32 degrees and boiling is at 212, a spread of 180 degrees. We don't argue about who's right; we either use the Fahrenheit paradigm or Celsius paradigm. You can focus on the differences or you can focus on what's similar. But one thing is true: the Celsius paradigm is part of the metric system embraced by the world but not by the U.S.A. So Americans have learned how to convert from one to the other. It would be silly to hang on to a way of thinking about temperature, melting and freezing points and not work together to speak the same language. We have formulas to make it easy. We can learn to be interested in how something works, and how we can communicate about it instead of defending our paradigm.

Now reflect on your relationships. Your paradigms filter

and interpret information and experience as good, bad, rude, helpful, useful, and difficult. Because paradigms are the filter or lens we look through, we often forget we are looking through anything at all. We assume that what we see, think, and feel is it. The obvious is so obvious that few people will look any further. Those same people that so confound you—co-workers, family members, organizational teams—can operate from very different paradigms, causing conflict when you're stuck with the notion that your paradigm is the right way or the only way. Then you might leave a job or a relationship because you don't know how to shift your paradigm to "see" and appreciate someone beyond your interpretation of who they are. And then we wonder why fulfillment can be so elusive in relationships.

Here's a simple fulfillment practice: Observe people you get along with, who are not reacting to a person who is difficult for you. Then ask them what they see. You can even ask them to coach you. It doesn't mean you're wrong, but it can move you to question the way you are responding to another person who is consistently difficult for you.

Why even bother with so much self-reflection? You want to notice what happens around people who are difficult for you so you can be more effective and aware of what triggers your reactions. If you're only effective with certain styles of people you will limit your ability to communicate effectively and produce results. Engaging in self-reflection about this now may allow the possibility of having more fulfilling relationships and less stress!

When you're in a state of self-reflection and not in a state of reaction, you can engage with clarifying questions, ask what's possible, and then move into action. What's the difference? Reaction is often shooting from the hip based on your existing paradigm. Reaction is inside of what you know. Remember this: it's what you know that got you into the situation, and it's not necessarily going to get you out. A new way of being in thoughts, words, and actions requires getting outside the box of your paradigm. A strong sense of curiosity can inspire self-reflection, mindfulness, and a lifelong practice of learning.

Intentional Change

How do you gain access to your own paradigms, to your own design, so you can intentionally change and be more effective? Most often we want to change the other person, and I think we can quickly come to the realization that's probably not going to happen!

You can shift your patterns of behavior by catching yourself in the act of reaction, and instead, just notice, watch, observe both yourself and the other person. This is what it means to be self-reflective. Change can happen as a result of your commitment to just notice when you're effective and fulfilled, and when you're not.

A friend of mine related his experience of "just noticing" when he had a potential altercation with his buddy of many years. I call it a "potential" altercation because it didn't come to pass. My friend sees himself as a responsible person, and his buddy as a freewheeling person not so concerned with convention or the consequences of his actions. Their past conversations had often ended in them not seeing each other for a while. But something happened on this particular occasion. My friend saw his "responsible" paradigm in action and stopped his reaction. Instead of giving his buddy a familiar lecture he realized he didn't want to continue that historical pattern and it immediately changed the tone and focus of the conversation and brought them both present to who they are now.

It's important to recognize your own paradigms for dealing with people. One way is to pay attention to your own rules and discover other people's rules. Remember your paradigms are a set of rules and regulations that determine the boundaries of your thinking and impact the actions you consider taking. Rules define the way you play the game of life, business, and relationships. They are the behavioral imperatives by which you assume everybody should play.

Rules, your rules, are not usually seen as arbitrary. Family, teachers, society, and experience had a hand in shaping them. When you discover any limiting or perhaps inappropriate paradigms you get access to your own mental design. It's challenging, but you begin by questioning their value to you and their value to others. You begin to notice whether they bring happiness and fulfillment for you and your relationships. You begin to notice whether they contribute to a life worth living.

It's interesting to note that often the first time someone is self-reflective is when everything they know to do in a given situation doesn't work. I believe that is the power and the opportunity in a problem you don't know how to solve. There's power in saying, "I don't know." It causes you to stop, reflect, and consider what's possible.

I know a manager, who had two people working for him who didn't get along and it was impacting their team. He invited them into his office and told them they were effective, capable people and he knew they could resolve whatever was going on with them. He didn't know what the solution was, but he held his people as capable of dealing with it. Their conflict was getting in the way of the project. In fact, people stopped inviting them to the same meetings. Isn't that what we do sometimes with difficult people? We hope it will go away or we avoid it by not having them in the same room at the same time. Does that really avoid it? No. It just prolongs the agony.

Their manager's commitment to the project and to his team was bigger than the conflict. He knew that conflict-like problems occur. That's why he brought them into his office. Put two people together over time and there will be conflict and often a clash of paradigms, of competing rules.

He told them he wasn't letting them out of his office until they resolved it. He had a very good relationship with both of these people and they respected him. So they sat down together and discussed what happened. Their conflict began months before, around a disagreement on an important course of action. The action had been implemented and was long over, but the residue of conflict remained. At the core of their conflict were competing paradigms.

One's paradigm, his set of rules, said you argue for what you believe. A person isn't committed to what they won't argue for, what they won't stand up for, he believed. He respected people who argue.

The other person's paradigm said arguing is rude. Arguing is an attempt to dominate. Arguing equals the end of a relationship. Arguing means you don't like me and you don't respect me. When they explored what caused the conflict it wasn't that they disagreed over the solution; it was how they communicated with each other. They had different expectations about the way people should be when they communicate. They had a competing set of paradigms about communication. On this day they listened to each other generously and emerged from their manager's office with a greater understanding of each other, and recognized their own set of rules on how people should communicate. Their awareness increased and their attachment to how people should communicate decreased.

The project got back on course. Sometimes all it takes is sitting down with a coach who is committed to resolution and who can create in others a commitment to listen and understand. A relationship can be strengthened through conflict, and through disagreement, if it's resolved. A conflict can focus a person's attention on differences. If you can use conflict to focus your attention, the difference can be addressed and resolved. Notice the effect you have on other people. Listen longer, ask more questions, appreciate differences, know yourself, and you will be more effective.

Don't let conflict escalate into people calling each other names. The least of which is that others are difficult! If you hear statements like "They're too aggressive," "They're so defensive," "They're rude," "They're irrational," "They're overly emotional," instead ask what happened, what specifically. Listen and encourage the person to deal with the situation. If you say nothing it may appear that you agree.

Some years ago, I was working with a department in a city government and was conducting pre-coaching interviews before I started a training program with them. I wanted to find out what was missing for people in their daily performance and in their overall results. I was speaking to a gentleman and discovered he had an ongoing conflict with another person in the department for over ten years. When I asked him to define the problem, he couldn't even remember what the problem was or how it started. He only knew that today the conflict continued. He couldn't be in the same meeting, work on the same projects, or even join the same professional associations as this other person. Everyone knew about the conflict but no one did anything about it. It had gotten to the point where he looked at his future with dread.

This is what he told me: "Another five years I'll retire and then it will be over." I responded that five years sounded too long to be in a position where you're not free to take action, be yourself, and be fulfilled. It's like being in prison for five years. Your ability to move is constricted. Something shifted for him when he began to see that he was in a kind of prison, and that it was a prison of his own design. I asked him what would be available to him if he gave up the limiting story about the other person. He was quiet for a while and then said, "I don't know. I've carried this around for so long." What we accomplished that day was a commitment on his part to just consider that resolution might be possible.

I was continuing my interviews the next day and I got a call from his wife. She said, "What did you do to my husband?" And then she continued and said, "I want to let you know what happened. If you don't do anything else but what you did for my husband, you will have done an outstanding service." He had taken my request seriously and considered the idea that resolution was possible. She told me, "My husband came home after you spoke with him and he called this man that he'd had a conflict with over the last ten years. He called and asked him to have lunch. During lunch he asked if they could end the conflict and the other man said yes. He couldn't remember how it originated either."

She then added, "Do you know that my husband has been complaining about this person for ten years and has hated to get up to go to work? This is a miracle." Now she continued to say that not only did he call his co-worker, he also called his children. He'd been having some conflict with them. And her kids called her back later that day and said, "Mom, what's going on with Dad? Is he dying?" They called because his conversations had the sound of someone who was putting the past to rest.

When you can bring completion to the past, it is a clear indication you are giving more importance to the resolution than to the conflict. Then you're free. Free to create the future unencumbered by the past. You stop waiting.

There's an old question "Would you rather be right or healed?" This man chose to be healed and when he was healed, so was the other man. It was one of those days I'll always cherish because I witnessed a powerful paradigm shift—the shift from being right to being complete.

The practice of uncovering your paradigms gives you access to what you hold to be true. Hold it lightly so you can discover what's outside the box of your current thinking and gain insight into views that hold more possibilities for you and others.

Practice: *Make your goal to say at the end of each day, "I'm complete in my conversations and actions." Say what you need to say to others from a commitment to resolution especially with people who are difficult for you.*

Design your words and actions to make a difference in your fulfillment, the results you produce, and in your relationships. Then you can get a good night's sleep and be present for the next moment, the next conversation, and the next day.

Solutions to Puzzles:

1. Solve the problem of connecting all 9 dots, without lifting your pencil off the paper, by going outside of the box formed by the nine dots.

2. Turn a IX into a 6 by adding an S ... a curved line.

SIX

Chapter 21

What You Focus On Prospers

"In order to succeed you must know what you're doing, love what you're doing, and believe in what you're doing." Will Rogers

My daughter asked me not too long ago what was important in a relationship. She asked me, "Is it love?" I thought about it for a while. Love is the obvious answer. Love is the key to building lasting relationships. Yet there is another ingredient. What keeps people together over time, whether it's a personal relationship or a group of people that work together, is a shared vision. If you have love and a shared vision where you're aiming in the same direction, you have a powerful combination that is fulfilling and builds relationships, achieves goals, and handles whatever problems show up day to day.

Vision and goals aim your energy and focus. What you focus on prospers and grows.

I have a friend who has come to the end of one career, a life giving and ministering to others. From where I sit he has always manifested his vision. And yet he is at a new beginning questioning his emerging vision for the next phase of his personal and professional growth. He acknowledges the success of his endeavors. He also sees the failures and missed opportunities. He has reviewed his life and seen threads of dreams that are enticing, and at the same time, unimportant for him at this stage. He's in the space between an ending and a new beginning.

The space between an ending and a new beginning is a fertile time to be with the question of what's fulfilling no matter your age or circumstance.

If you find yourself at this juncture, you may want to consider keeping a journal. Make some notes. Ask yourself the question over a cup of coffee in the morning. Light a candle and sit with the question. Just ask with no concern for the answer and see what comes to mind. What inspires you? Don't block any ideas just because you think they're impossible. Let every answer come. Keep asking and with every response tell yourself "thank you!" and continue asking the question. This practice allows you to accept the idea as a possibility and with every thank you you're opening up a little more space to explore your vision unencumbered by pre-existing notions, judgments, conditions, circumstances, your past, your job, your education, and timing.

If you have a valued coach, a dialogue around fulfillment can be very revealing. Stay in the conversation with your coach long enough to move beyond all your known responses like more money, travel, new career, or a relationship. Don't ignore those responses but go further and ask what fulfillment money, travel, new career, or a relationship will bring. Just ask the question and let your genuine responses reveal what's meaningful to you now. Love is an essential ingredient because when you love what you're doing you attract relationships, information, and opportunities that make a difference.

Notice where you place your focus on a day-to-day basis. One day on my drive to work I noticed that I started thinking of negative consequences like what would happen if we didn't achieve our sales volume, or if a valued associate resigned or if we missed a deadline. I caught myself in the act of creating and worrying about negative outcomes. I was focused on outcomes I didn't want. This is different from recognizing a problem and facing the problem head-on to discover what's possible. I noticed what I was doing and it triggered a question. I wondered what was gained by producing negative outcomes in my mind. Actually I asked myself what the hell was I thinking! What was that kind of thinking going to produce?

I stopped and intervened in the "negative outcome thinking" by asking myself the following coaching questions: "If you're going to focus on fulfillment, how do you want it to be? What do you need to be focused on to achieve the result you intend?" In order to succeed you must know what you're doing and what you want so you can focus.

And, lo and behold, possibilities would flow in my seven-minute drive to the office, so by the time I arrived I was entertaining a solution versus being bombarded by problems. I was thinking forward. And in the next breath, I asked myself what was driving my concern. Instead of ignoring the concern, I identified it and thought about what action I needed to take to resolve it. The impact on my team was visible as soon as I walked in the door. If I can come up with possibilities so can they. If I can confront issues so can they. This is the heart of building relationships that don't fall apart when you have problems. This is the power of moving forward from a shared vision and focusing on what you want to achieve.

Coaching

Have you ever noticed that as soon as you can't see any possibilities you tend to leave a situation because you don't know how to be successful? And what you'll be left with is a story about why it didn't work. An effective coach will intervene in the stories you tell yourself by questioning what limits you, leading you to consider what will give you the power to hold in mind what you want and take the necessary steps to make it so.

If you pick up a business journal today, you'll most likely find an article on coaching or on managers who are using coaching in their organizations. More and more people are learning coaching skills. However, in talking to individuals and managers across the country they'll say they think about coaching to help them access their vision or accomplish their goals, but they're not sure whether they do it or even whether they really know what it is.

When I've asked different managers "What is required to be an effective coach?" the responses are similar. They say it is someone who is genuinely committed, who holds people accountable for the promises they make; someone who is consistent and even-handed in their approach; someone who is non-judgmental and doesn't go nuclear or explode or withdraw when problems are revealed. It's someone who confronts the issues and is able to get you involved in solving problems, setting goals, and improving your performance. Your coach is someone who cares about the results and about you; about your fulfillment both in achieving what you set out to do and being fulfilled along the way.

Great coaches don't tell you what to do. They inspire you to move past limitations in your thinking. They listen in a special way. They listen for commitment. Who is a coach for you? What do they bring to the relationship? Think about the people in your life that have been coaches for you. What were they like when they were coaching you? If they were memorable, they were probably the people committed to your success. They got you to focus on what you wanted instead of what you didn't want. This is an extraordinary practice.

I listen carefully to what people say. In fact when people tell me what they don't want, I say, "Thank you. What do you want?" Often they'll continue telling me what they don't want. Why? If you said what you wanted you might have to go for it, get committed, and make a plan. You might fail! That's the difference between a fantasy and a vision. Saying what you don't want keeps you from declaring what you do want and prevents you from focusing on it, which is the first step to attracting it into your life.

Are you coachable?

This is an important question. Sometimes people will ask for coaching but they're not coachable. This may be an indication that they're not willing to confront their stories or create the time they need to get something done.

To be coached you must confront the unknown and not be afraid to fail. This is really the footprint of a confident person. Confidence doesn't come from always being right; it comes from not being afraid of failure. So if the answer is that you are coachable, how do you know when to get a fulfillment coach? In situations where you don't see possibilities or you just need someone to make a commitment to, it's important to ask for coaching. In the act of getting a coach you ask for help and move your focus to what you want.

You may need a coach to help you let go of your attachment to an outcome when it gets in the way of your performance. If you're not getting buy-in from others, it may be time to notice whether you are attempting to force agreement. It's hard to give up attachment to your ideas and solutions. If you get attached to your ideas and you need to get the buy-in of others, you may find resistance instead of agreement. Giving up attachment to being right leads to finding a solution that works for all concerned.

Attachment intensifies when you would rather be right than be in the unknown or out of control. But that's where breakthroughs happen—at the edge of what you already know. You focus on what you want and then let go of attachment to the outcome, so you can bring your full attention present to plan strategies, take action, and build relationships.

Getting a fulfillment coach, a committed partner, starts with a request. Ask some treasured friends to read this book with you and discover their vision of a life worth living. Be fulfillment coaches for each other. You can have different fulfillment coaches for different goals. My daughter and I are coaches for each other on our health and weight. We coach each other to be fulfilled and keep each other on course. And the best part is we're having fun and keeping fit! Fulfillment is a no-excuse mentality. Feedback about what we eat, how often we exercise, and what the scale says informs new action, not excuses. The feedback gives us a way to measure our progress; it does not become an excuse for why it won't work.

Do you ever watch coaches at sporting events? They never get on the field and look at the opposing team and say, "They're just too big. They haven't lost a game all season and we've lost games, so we're not going to play today." Coaches do not give up. They don't give up on the results and they don't give up on you. They have a way of holding you as capable. In fact, they often see a possibility in you that you may not see … yet.

The Core Of A Committed Coaching Relationship

1. A shared vision that organizes your actions day after day and sustains fulfillment through mistakes and breakdowns.
2. A clear understanding that you can only coach commitment, and be coached if you're committed to your goals. (Commitment transcends wants, desires, good ideas, talent or inclinations.)
3. A vow to never give up on yourself, the vision, or each other.

Practice: *Notice today what you focus on. Is what you focus on what you want to achieve?*

Would coaching move you forward in the direction of your vision of a life worth living?

Fulfillment coaches prepare you to believe in yourself, your abilities, and your readiness for surprises, obstacles, and challenges along the way. They don't do it for you; they see you as capable of being fulfilled and fulfilling your goal. Fulfillment coaches manage by commitment, by the promises you make. Not by what they expect, but what you promise you will do. That's the essence of a committed relationship.

Chapter 22

A Committed Relationship

"The dedicated life is the life worth living." Annie Dillard

I've realized time after time that you can only coach people who are committed to achieving a goal or having a breakthrough in their performance, whether personal or professional … no matter how talented they are. I think it has to be something they want to do that's fulfilling and satisfying, and in some way aligned with their original promise … their vision of a life worth living.

Have you ever tried to talk someone into doing something? No matter how much you support the idea, if they're not committed to the goal, they won't achieve it or will approach it half-heartedly or just do it for you!

I'm reminded of this fact of life in organizations, in families, and in relationships. On the job you can demand someone's time but you can't demand his or her commitment. You can't demand that someone be happy or committed to what you want. You can only coach someone's commitment. And when you do, fulfillment is possible right from the beginning, in the conception of the idea with the declaration of intention and vision.

Commitment is the path to extraordinary results and experiencing fulfillment along the way.

How does a committed partnership or a fulfillment coach move you forward? What does a coach do? The coach's job is to ensure clarity of your vision and goals, and support your performance throughout the process. A coach guides a clear focus during the cycle of fulfillment, including course changes and corrections along the way. A coach moves you away from the cycle of disappointment, knowing there is always more to learn and new solutions to discover when mistakes or breakdowns occur. Coaches also realize the personal growth that occurs when people take on something outside of what they already know how to do.

Finding A Coach

If you're looking for a coach, find someone who believes in you and what you're doing. Someone who is honest with you, gives you feedback, holds you accountable for what you say you will do, stands with you against obstacles, and celebrates your victories; someone who understands and supports your goals and why they are important to you.

You can share a goal with another person and coach each other. Be aware that you can have the same goal but you may be involved for different reasons. Don't assume that everyone has the same interests as you. Someone may take on a goal for the prize. Someone else may take on the goal to expand her body of knowledge, someone else for social approval, while another may commit to a goal to make a difference. Two people could share a weight loss goal, one to look good and the other for health reasons. One isn't better than the other. People have different interests and different values. What is fundamental is that whatever your reasons are for taking on the goal, it's your goal. It's your vision. It ignites your passion.

When a company I co-founded was acquired, it was a key initiative to keep the management team. The founder and I were accountable for the success of the acquisition. We believed in it and knew that it would bring the necessary capital, expansion, and synergies that would serve the vision of the organization. A member of our team left after only thirty days with the new organization. He'd been with the company over five years, starting as an analyst and had grown in responsibility, heading up four departments. His interest was growth and learning. He left for a new job where his title was actually a step down, but the opportunity to expand his knowledge and grow in new areas was extensive, making the decision to leave the company easier.

From his perspective, it looked as though his present job would be narrowly focused on his current skill set without the opportunity for growth. His personal vision was aligned in the old company, but not in the new company. I realized that a key step was missing in the acquisition process: Sitting down with each person and asking them questions about whether their vision and goals were aligned in the new enterprise and if not, what would make a difference? A commitment to develop people doesn't stop regardless of how long they've been in the organization.

Sometimes business leaders want to hurry through development plans where individuals set goals, if they do development plans at all. As a business leader, manager, or coach you work with your people to create goals to improve performance; you sit down and coach them to create a well-aimed goal; a goal that is in alignment with their raison d'etre— their original promise—as well as meeting the company goals. Then the process of creation will be illuminating and you will come up with real goals that move both the organization and the individual forward. If you manage other people and you don't take the time to coach and develop them, you miss the opportunity to build a culture of fulfillment. Coaching allows you to focus on performance, develop talent, and make the hard decision to release players who don't get results … often because they're not fulfilled or committed in what they're doing.

On the job each person needs to know the vision and goals of the organization. It sometimes floors me that businesspeople talk about "silos," where some departments don't know how what they do fits into the whole picture. Their bonuses are geared toward what they accomplish, even if it's at the detriment of other areas of the company. So manufacturing will inflate their price to a division or ship in merchandise at the end of the year to make their goals and inflate that division's inventory at the end of the year. Oy vey! How does this happen? How do you have an organization operating as a whole and not as parts, each one operating in their own self-interest?

Committed relationships are interdependent. Your ownership as the executive/manager/coach is to hold the person and department accountable to the whole so you can foster fulfillment and achieve goals.

Have you ever coached someone who loved what they did? And did you notice that even the most menial of tasks were done with care and full attention? When you love what you do there's equanimity with all of it. There's a sense that the action fits together like a puzzle and you remain interested and connected from the beginning when everything is possible, and in the middle when dealing with obstacles, and all the way to the end when you can say, "I am complete and grateful for all of it."

Practice: *If you are a coach or manager, use the following questions to establish a committed relationship and learn more about the people you work with every day. You can ask:*

"What do you want to achieve ... both personally and professionally?"

"Where do you see yourself in the next two to three years?"

"What do you feel you need to improve?"

"What are some possible goals you can set that would accelerate your progress?"

"What does fulfillment look like for you?"

"What are you passionate about?"

Through this dialogue you come to a point where individuals are ready to consider and declare powerful and fulfilling goals for the organization and for themselves.

Chapter 23

Coaching Fulfillment

"Without a deadline, I wouldn't do nothing, baby!" Louis Armstrong

Do you notice that when you don't set a deadline it's hard to finish or to track your success? I bet that when you're coaching others' fulfillment you check in on their progress. You don't get to the next conversation, performance appraisal, or meeting and say, "Yeah, whatever happened to that goal?" When you come to the end of the creation phase you ask the person you're coaching, "Are you committed to this goal? Are you doing this for the right reasons … because it matters and is fulfilling?" If the response is yes, you sign off on the goal.

If the goal is yours, the process is the same. "Are you committed to the goal? Do you understand the motivation, intention, and vision that inspired this goal?" If the answer is yes to all these questions, you move into the next phase; if not you return to the beginning and stay longer in the question "What is my vision of a life worth living?" The answer to that question informs the goals you set. Without clarity on the meaning behind the goals, and why it's important to you, what you seek can show up half-baked with a recipe for incompletion.

Sometimes people will get through creation and even plan the actions, but don't set a time frame, so they get to the routine of their day and the important, fulfilling goal they just declared can slip into a fantasy. I'll say it again because it's essential to manifestation.

Without a time frame there is no commitment.

Fulfillment coaches manage by commitment. Think about this scenario: You need an analysis of an unbudgeted marketing expense you think will produce a significant return for your business. You leave a meeting thinking that not only was a course of action established, but also everyone knew their role and the timeline by when it must be completed. Then you check back when the report was due only to be told, "Oh, I don't have it done yet." And you say, "Well, I said I needed to get it done." And then they say, "Well, I thought you understood that I had another project to finish."

Phrases like "right away," "next week," and "ASAP" sound like we would all know what that means. Someone says, "I need it right away." So what do you ask when you're managing by commitment? What you ask is, "When specifically do you need it?" So let's say they come back with, "Well, as soon as possible." When you're managing by commitment you say, "Okay, give me a time and date." Persist. You can't give a committed response without knowing the deadline. Once you know the time frame you can say yes or no or offer another possibility.

Sometimes people will tell me they don't want to push. If you think asking is pushing you may believe that if you communicate clearly and state directly what you need that you qualify as "pushy". I'd suggest you consider a new definition of asking as saying something in order to obtain an answer or some information. You don't have to be pushy, just ask the questions without attachment to the response. Together you'll find the answer that is appropriate to getting things done. You may have to help someone set their priorities, or bring in additional resources so you can get done what needs to be done.

I sometimes find, when an apparently agreed-upon action doesn't happen, it reveals a lack of agreement in the first place. Remember the chapter on broken agreements? One of the most productive questions to ask when an agreed-upon action doesn't happen is "Did we have an agreement?" You may be surprised when the answer to this question is no, whether it's your boss, mate, spouse, friend, partner, or children answering the question!

I have coached people continuously in this one principle. I call it the "by when?" principle. It's managing by commitment rather than managing by expectation. There's no commitment until someone says yes and by when. Remember the conflict of expectations? You can't hold people accountable for your expectations. You can only hold them accountable for what they promise to do, and a promise includes a time frame.

It's also important in the manifestation phase, when you're planning action and getting commitment, to find out whether the plan requires additional resources—money, time, or people. What kind of help will you need? You may need to make a request. Sometimes we hold off making requests until the last minute. Why? We don't know what to do next if people say no. It takes practice to make requests. Once you start practicing it's like anything else you practice—playing tennis, learning a sport, speaking French—you improve with dedicated practice. One of the blocks to fulfillment is not asking for help when you need it. All you need is to be able to articulate your request and have the stamina to hear a no.

I had an experience with a close associate at work who had exhausted all her strategies for helping a terminated employee with her healthcare policy. I asked her to call the insurance company and request that the account executive call the employee and look at what was possible. My associate said that the account executive wouldn't call, it wouldn't work, he wouldn't have time, and they'd already done everything that could be done. I've worked with my associate for a long time. I've been a coach for her for ten years. So I could easily say and did, "Don't say no for the account executive, just make the request." She got it. She picked up the phone, made the call, and the account executive, without a moment's hesitation, said yes.

Hold others as capable of saying yes and no authentically. Plan the requests you need to make and make them. Don't say no for others. A conversation for action often starts with a request. A well-planned request is clear, directed at someone capable of fulfilling the request, and includes a timeline. A well-planned request allows clarifying questions and an inquiry into what, why, where, when, and how.

I'm reminded often of the importance of this skill and practice. A friend I worked with for many years went to a different organization (a Fortune 500 blue-chip company), and this is what he told me about his new job: "They don't make requests. It drives me crazy. People talk about what they want to do, but are afraid to make requests because it seems so confrontational." It is confrontational. It confronts the opportunity to tell the truth and listen with compassion. It confronts the opportunity to open up a dialogue or get feedback on your ideas.

In the creation phase it may seem easy because in creation you're imagining the outcome and you haven't run into any obstacles. In this practice of fulfillment, it's important to ask what kind of obstacles you or others might run into and plan accordingly. You don't bring up obstacles to move yourself or others off the goal or to be negative. You bring them up in the planning stage so you can be prepared; you design strategies to overcome the obstacles and you design help if it's needed.

In the manifestation phase you do the kind of planning that will put people into action with a time frame to achieve the goal. When you sign off on the plan, you are saying that you are convinced the plan is sufficient, and you and others are not only in action, but are capable of achieving the goal. Once the plan is created, obstacles are discussed, and time frames are established, follow-up is required. I like to do commitment checks with myself and others. A commitment check says we're committed to the plan.

If you're coaching people this is a critical step. You set up the follow-up and don't leave things to chance. Follow-up needs to be done as part of the manifestation phase. If you don't plan the follow-up sessions, they can easily fall by the wayside. Too often you get to the next meeting and that is the first time you check in on the progress you or your people are making. Don't make that mistake as the coach, whether coaching yourself or others. You're not only getting commitment from your people, you are making a commitment of your own, and that commitment is shown by your interest and follow-up. If you don't care about what's being accomplished, it will be difficult to follow up with interest. Research shows that attention and follow-up help people break through to new levels of performance; they accomplish more of their goals. Not a surprise! In order for follow-up to be effective, vision and goals have to be clearly defined.

Clarity on the goal puts you in action. Follow-up ensures it gets fulfilled. Can you imagine a coach not following up? When you're the coach, follow-up demonstrates your interest and communicates that the goals are important.

I realized early on in life that I could learn anything when I devoted time and attention to it. What often started as awkwardness, over time became part of my knowledge bank. At first you're in a learning phase, but later you become skillful. You learn from others when you're coachable and if you're coachable you can learn from everyone and every situation.

One of my first bosses said something to me I'll never forget. He said, "People don't care how much you know until they know how much you care." Think about the people you know that make demands, give the answers, and make all the decisions. Even if they're highly talented and the decisions are sound, if they don't care about the people around them, if they don't pay attention to them, listen to them, or value them, people leave.

If coaching fulfillment were easy, everyone would be doing it. If you're going to create a relationship that matters, you have to be able to tell the truth with compassion. Think about the times you say things that limit you. Maybe it's the path of least resistance to stay in the excuse instead of forging new ground. Until someone says, "Did you hear what you just said?" you may not actually think about why you're arguing for what you don't want, or putting blocks between you and another person.

Recently a manager said to me, "I don't have any concerns coaching people who come to me with problems, but what about the person you know is stuck with a problem and is going to miss a deadline but won't ask for help? In fact, they're not telling me about it at all." We already know not asking for help is a block to fulfillment. Now what do you do? Do you pretend you don't know? No. What you do instead is approach and say, "I understand we've got a problem to solve. We've got a conflict to deal with. Help me understand the problem. What happened?" Remember, you're empowering people to come up with their own answers, but you're also there to declare breakdowns or potential breakdowns when or before they occur. Don't pretend it's not happening or wait until time is up to act! People might say when you approach them, "Well, I didn't want to bother you," or "I was working on it," or "Actually I have it figured out." Sometimes all that needs to happen is to let them know that you're there as a resource in a timely fashion.

What's beneficial about recognizing breakdowns is the opportunity to revisit your vision. Vision reminds you why you are doing what you're doing.

Breakdowns happen in the cycle of fulfillment.

Breakdowns force you to deal with problems when they first occur, otherwise you couldn't accomplish the goal, achieve the result, and be fulfilled.

There's a great example of this when NASA sent the space shuttle Endeavour on its maiden voyage. Its mission was to retrieve a stranded satellite and relaunch it to its intended geosynchronous orbit. There was a limited amount of time in which they could retrieve that satellite. The job of 2 astronauts was to walk in space and attach a capture bar to the satellite so they could bring it on board. No matter what they did they couldn't get it attached. It was in the newspaper each day—were they going to have to abort their mission, or were they going to be able to do it given the time frame they had to confront the problem? What the astronauts did broke the rules. The decision was made to send 3 astronauts on a record breaking and unplanned space walk. It was the first time that 3 astronauts, from the same spacecraft, walked in space at the same time. And the result? The 3 of them were able to maneuver the satellite back to the shuttle so the capture bar could be attached.

Effective people are not afraid of limits or breakdowns. They know the old rules may not work. They know confronting a limit can snap people out of complacency and cause a breakthrough. They're comfortable dealing with conflict. They're willing to declare a breakdown. When you're trusted as a coach, leader, parent, or partner, others will look to you to put an issue on the table, to actually declare the breakdown so you can achieve the outcome you want.

Fulfillment coaching is a relationship that can be formal or informal. You'll know someone is a coach for you because you break through to new levels of performance and you feel better around them … you feel more alive with increased possibilities; you'll know because they often rattle the cage of your thinking so you can take new action that moves you toward your vision of a life worth living.

Practice: *Be a fulfillment coach.*

Fulfillment coaching changes who you are and how you think about what's reachable. Quite simply, if you're a manager, you need to coach in order to develop yourself and the people around you effectively, with intention and foresight. That's part of what you do every day if you're working in business, or in life, to achieve what you say you want and be fulfilled.

You'll know you're a coach when you stop what you're doing when there's a problem and listen. You're not giving the answer, but giving the space to look, to inquire, and together come up with a strategy that works. And if you work for the same organization, you coach someone to come up with a strategy that produces intended results for the company.

Listening instead of answering also works at home!

Chapter 24

Advice, Feedback, And Problem Solving

"The essence of action is accomplishment. To accomplish means to unfold something into the fullness of its essence." Martin Heidegger

There are three areas that you may find yourself engaged in daily, whether you're a manager, parent, friend, or business owner. You will be giving advice, feedback, and solving problems. You'll also be listening to the same. So how is fulfillment coaching different from advice, feedback, and problem solving?

Advice

Let's look at advice first. Sometimes people think coaching is giving people advice, having a heart-to-heart. With advice you can generally be assured that there is no commitment. People might ask for advice but are reluctant to receive it. They really want commiseration, which is a formula for co-misery!

Remember, fulfillment coaching is a committed relationship, both on the part of the person coaching and the person being coached.

Your commitment in being coached is you will do what you say, and keep the promises you make. You will perform and implement the actions you promise to take, and continue until you reach the finish line.

As a fulfillment coach your commitment is to receive another's promise as an active partner and coach all the way through the completion of the goal. A coach doesn't exit mid-game. When you're giving advice it's like a drive-by suggestion!

When you make a commitment to me as your coach, I am actively engaged in accepting your promise. I make sure it is in a time frame that works, that obstacles have been discussed and overcome. When I sign off on the goal, I am adding my conscious support and follow-up. I'm holding you as ready, willing, and able. I'm holding your success in mind. I believe in you and in your goals. I know that the goal is in alignment with your original promise—with who you are—and your vision of a life worth living.

In a coaching relationship, if people take on too ambitious of a goal or too ambitious of a time frame and you let them do it without any questions, you're demonstrating a lack of interest or skill. Or you may have a concern about telling someone the truth of what you see. As a fulfillment coach you know the limits of your skills. If the coaching opportunity is outside your realm of experience, you can guide someone to an expert. You don't give advice; instead, you listen with interest.

If you are the one being coached, you realize that the coach isn't there to do your thinking for you, or to take the action. They are there to ask questions and give you a framework to think through your commitments before you make them.

The framework includes a structure for fulfillment and is managed by commitment. The coach asks for people to mean it when they say yes. If you want people to say yes and mean it, they must also have the option of saying no. So if you're guiding someone to a goal and you hear a half-hearted response rather than a clear yes, you can use that as an opening for further discussion. For instance you can ask, "Well, what's the hesitation?" and find out whether there's anything in the way of them accomplishing that goal. Is it fear or disinterest? If you're giving advice instead of asking questions and listening, the response is often half-hearted because you haven't gotten to someone else's commitment. Advice is about you reflecting your ideas.

Think about the times when you have given advice. How was the advice received? Often advice causes the listener to tell a story about why that advice won't work, or how someone else has already tried that and it didn't work. There's no commitment to explore what's possible and there's no commitment on the part of the person giving the advice to partner and coach. Advice is part of the expectation cycle; the "let me tell you what to do" style of management, parenting, or partnership. This doesn't mean coaches can't offer possibilities or options, they can and they do. But they have conversations about what's possible and leave people in action to explore their vision with a commitment of true ownership. If you're a coach and you're doing all the talking, you may want to stop and ask more questions and listen.

Feedback

How is coaching different from feedback? Feedback is an important part of fulfillment coaching. Feedback is information. Coaching takes the feedback to another level. Coaching leaves people in action. Feedback leaves people with information. Coaching deepens the impact of feedback. I encourage people every day to hear feedback as information instead of criticism. When you make that shift in the way you listen, you can ask questions rather than argue about who's right or wrong. You can stop feeling demeaned by the information, even when it sounds critical. Questions like "What happened?" or "How did you come to that conclusion?" or "Hmm, I didn't think about it that way. What is possible now?" have the power to shift feedback into useful information.

Have you ever received a performance appraisal? If you're like most people, you want them because in the best of times they're tied to getting a financial increase and in the worst of times you want to find out what's working and what's not working. Still, you might tell me that performance appraisals are generally empty. You are often given the information and that's it. In contrast, a coaching relationship moves you into action to sort through the feedback to make course corrections.

Feedback is worthless if there's no opportunity to integrate the information into your performance. When you move feedback into action, you'll have the opportunity to self-correct and be successful. If you're the coach, you don't expect someone to integrate the feedback by chance; you get their commitment to do it. They create a practice of improvement, not out of fear of failure, but out of a commitment to be fulfilled and achieve your goals.

Problem Solving

How's coaching different from problem solving? Have you noticed that one of the main roles of people in business and life is to solve problems? However, if you are solving all of the problems that your mate, family, friends, or business associates are bringing you then you are missing the point of a relationship that matters. If you're a manager, you have a primary role in developing the people you work with. Not just for the sake of development, but for the sake of accomplishing the vision and goals of the company.

Have you ever witnessed the following scenario? A manager goes in to tell her boss a problem and before she gets it all out, the boss is in action to solve it by telling her what to do. Meanwhile she is saying, "Wait a minute. I haven't told you what I've already done. I handled it."

When people bring you a problem as a manager, parent, or friend (and especially with loved ones), one of the most valuable things you can do is ask questions and assist them in thinking through the problem. That's how we learn and grow. You don't do it for them; you spend the time with them so discovery can take place.

Colleagues have come into my office, faces flushed, to talk with me when they have problems and I'll ask, "What happened?" And then I listen and ask questions, such as "What has been done so far?" I want to make sure the right problem is being solved and the person who has the problem owns the solution.

One of my managers came into my office after a conversation with a customer that didn't go particularly well, and asked me to call the customer back. I asked her why she thought it would be better for me to call this person. She said that I had a good relationship with the person. That was true, and she also said that if there was any misunderstanding she believed I would be able to handle it; I would be able to fix it. I thought about her request and I considered it, but I realized that my making the callback wouldn't do anything for her relationship with the customer. So instead, I coached her to make the callback. Now what was the difference between my making the call and her making the call? The difference was the empowerment and development of a valued employee. Her making that call successfully saved me hours of calls in the future.

Several years later she left the organization and relocated to a different city. I was there to do a presentation and we had lunch and I met her new manager. He acknowledged how well she handled conflict and anticipated customers' concerns before they even happened. He was amazed and called it her "customer service radar." She looked at me and laughed saying, "I'd rather handle it once because then I don't have to make a callback." If I had solved the problem for her several years back, her manager would still be solving problems for her today.

A fulfillment coach asks questions to help people solve problems or correct mistakes. Questions like:

- What happened?
- What do you think is missing?
- What are some alternatives you've considered?
- What are some other possibilities for solving this problem?
- What do you think is the best option?
- Can you commit to that?
- What will you do?
- When will you do it?
- Do you anticipate any obstacles to implementing the solution?
- How can these obstacles be overcome?

By asking questions, a committed response is evoked, people learn how to think for themselves, and can be empowered and inspired to come up with and implement solutions. You are saying to them that you believe they're capable.

Now sometimes my associates will say, "Well, coaching takes time." Yes, it does take time. But the several hours or even the weeks you spend coaching someone through a problem will net you hundreds of hours in the future.

How does this idea line up with the notion that whenever people bring you a problem they should bring you a solution? What I've noticed in organizations is that people who come up with solutions usually implement them and what they bring you is the result. They'll come to you and say, "This is the problem we had. This is the solution we came up with. And this is the result we got." But what do you do when people have trouble coming up with the solution? Often I find that people who don't come up with solutions suffer. They may hide the problem, make excuses, or procrastinate. They may be afraid they'll come up with the wrong solution. They may even be afraid to come up with a recommendation, thinking that it won't be an effective resolution.

Problems put pressure on people to perform now, to perform immediately.

You want people to put the problem on the table. If they can't solve it they address the issue with you or put the problem front and center at a meeting so it can be resolved. Watch closely. A shift will begin to happen. The truth emerges.

I've been coaching executives and managers for many years and sometimes I'll get a call from a manager who will say, "I was picking up the phone to call you to coach me on a problem I'm having. And I started asking myself the coaching questions I knew you would ask me. And before long I'd solved the problem. So I'm calling you to report on my success." When this happens, I know the coaching principles and questions have become a self-generating conversation. Fulfillment coaching is part of who they are and becomes part of the company culture.

Practice: *Notice today whether you're coaching, giving advice, giving feedback or solving problems for others.*

Notice after any conversation if the person is in action and if the result of your conversation matched your intention.

In business and in life I've learned the tao of coaching: The mediocre coach tells, the good coach asks, the superior coach demonstrates, and the great coach inspires.

Chapter 25

Inquiry: The Art Of Asking Questions

"Love the questions and perhaps you'll live your way into the answers."
Rainer Maria Rilke

The art of asking questions is tied to how well you listen. Listening is the absence of planning what you're going to say, interpreting what's being said as right or wrong or just waiting in silence so you can say what's on your mind. Listening is the pathway to being fulfilled with another person. So how do you listen as a manager, coach, or friend so you can even ask a question and be interested in the response?

Non-defensively.

The secret is to suspend reaction so you can be present with a clear mind and heart to listen and discover what you don't already know.

As children we're taught to listen and we're reminded often to notice quickly when we're not listening and self-correct. So as adults, we should be masters at it. Right? Then you talk to adults who still have trouble listening. What's your internal conversation when you're not listening? Would it sound something like, "I don't want to hear this!" or "Don't tell me what to do," or "I've already decided." You may not actually say those words out loud but you're still listening through that interpretation, and it impacts what you hear and what you say in response.

The outcome is that you most likely resist the information, get defensive or offended, gloss over it or just shut down, no matter how carefully the message is delivered.

This reminds me of a funny story from Steve Martin. It goes like this: "There's now a sophisticated communication technique that eases marital strain and opens wide the doors of understanding between the sexes. This new technique developed by psychologists and sociologists is called … listening. It will be interesting to see whether this new technique will disappear and be replaced by older and more traditional techniques such as leaving the room."

I laugh out loud when I think about this story and how good we are at tuning out what we don't want to hear.

Listen Like It Matters

Listening is difficult, and yet it's crucial to a loving relationship. It's also essential on the job and when you're coaching or managing another person. So how do you listen? Wait to respond. Leave space for thinking. Consider what's being said. If you are doing all the talking, stop and take a breath. Ask a question and then wait for the response. Remember the key to the next question you ask is in what the person reveals.

Have your questions be an inquiry, not an inquisition. You are not interrogating people. Remember you're on their team. Design your questions to reveal and uncover possibilities, ownership, and commitment. Interrogation comes across as a relentless drive to a pre-determined point that only you know.

How will you know when you're interrogating instead of asking questions? Recognize when you don't wait for a response, or when you don't listen thoroughly before asking another question. Another good place to pay attention is when you are in a hurry to say what's on your mind. If you're asking one question right after another, you're most likely interrogating rather than asking. And this is especially obvious when the questions you ask don't really relate to what was just said. This is an indication you're thinking about what to say next, rather than listening to what's being said.

Silent pauses give you time to think about what's being said; to consider and respect the value others bring. Here's an exercise you can do to shift how you listen. Are you ready?

Take the next month and listen to other people, everyone, including your parents, even the people that are difficult for you, as if they were coaches for you.

Now sometimes, when I propose this, people start laughing as they consider that their mother could be a coach for them. And then it sinks in ... the way they listen to other people can and does determine their response in advance of any conversation.

If you think someone is a jerk, you don't consider what he or she has to say. I'm asking you to reverse your thinking. What you think about someone shapes how you listen to him or her. This is a revealing practice. If you can listen to others like they're coaches for you, you'll start to listen non-defensively and perhaps see something you haven't considered before. You can pause with a moment of silence and say, "Thank you. I'll think about that." You can listen, consider, and ask questions.

If you continue to think your response is tied to the way another person is talking or being, you're allowing yourself to be controlled by how someone speaks or acts. It's very freeing to find out that your response is yours and is determined by how you listen, not by how someone speaks.

The opportunity is to be present and listen the way you would like someone to listen to you.

Listening To Difficult People

You can check this out yourself. Notice where you have trouble listening because you think someone is difficult—perhaps you think they're obnoxious or abrasive in meetings—then ask someone else, "What did you think of the meeting?" without predisposing them to your opinion. You may be surprised. They might say, "Oh, I think that's just what we needed to hear." Remember, sometimes what we interpret as difficult is just a different communication style.

In these kinds of situations what can allow you to listen is to separate the message from the style. If you understand that different people have different styles and you're not controlled by how someone is communicating, you are free to hear what they have to say and respond to the message instead of the style. It is important for you to notice how you come across—remember the old adage that it's not what you say but how you say it—however, mastery depends on suspending your reaction to how someone is speaking to you so you can hear the message, ask questions and discover something new.

Listening Generously

There's a great deal of literature and training on communication, and yet in everyday life it's very challenging to create a "what's possible" environment, which is foundational to the art of inquiry and listening. It requires almost a moment-to-moment commitment to let go of attachment to any one position or pre-conceived answer and be committed to discovery and relationship. You can have strong opinions and still listen generously. The key is in being open to discover something you don't already know or something that might challenge your opinion.

If you're listening to someone you don't agree with, listen closely to what they are saying. You can get distracted by focusing on what you want to say instead of just listening, so you miss what someone is telling you. If you listen you will know what to say next. You'll often find a key question contained in what they're telling you if you just listen a little longer than you're comfortable.

Listening goes way beyond being able to paraphrase what someone just told you. It's the ability to get comfortable with silence so you can connect beyond the normal exchanges of what people say to each other. When you genuinely listen you can ask well-aimed questions that get to the heart of the matter and each other.

The art of asking questions is in how you listen. Ask yourself this question: "How do you want to be listened to?" I've asked groups and individuals on many occasions this very question. Most people say they just want to be heard. Being heard is not the same as agreement or disagreement. It means to consider what someone is saying as valuable. You won't always agree and in some instances may strongly disagree. The challenge is to listen and exchange ideas while inviting questions and keeping an inquiry alive.

Practice: *Listen to others the way you want to be listened to. Uncross your arms, lean forward, and engage.*

Chapter 26

Action: Managing By Commitment

"Discipline is practicing a thousand days. Refinement is practicing ten thousand days." 15th Century Samurai

The key to living a fulfilled life is to take your time and make sure your actions come from your vision of fulfillment. Who are you in action? What do you notice about yourself? Do you start and stop? Wait until all the conditions are perfect? Create a plan and stick to it with some things and not with others? Have an urgency to move into manifestation—to move into action? Is your credo "Let's just do something."

I encourage you to stay in creation a little longer in the area of your interest. Explore what's possible until a true commitment emerges. Enthusiasm can carry you for a while but won't sustain you like a true vision, with a considered and committed plan of action. If you ask for commitment before you've explored what's possible, you, along with others, may rush to a "first" response, which may not be the best goal or the best solution. Instead, examine a commitment that is both fulfilling and that produces a significant result. That's when you can move into sustainable action and begin managing by commitment. Managing time is a misnomer. You can only manage your commitments and that means managing what you say yes to.

Time wasted or well spent is a result of managing your commitments.

How do you discover your commitment? Goals need to be relevant and timely, groundbreaking and specific. Goals need to be meaningful for you and if at work, for the organization. The key to managing by commitment is being willing to tell the truth about where you're committed and where you're not. Once you know what you're committed to you can fulfill the goal and be fulfilled in the actions you take right now.

Even if you're in a state of "pre-clarity" or not knowing what to do in an area of your life that's important to you—see it as a discoverable process.

I've noticed in coaching people that when I say confusion is a state of pre-clarity it usually settles them down. They actually start laughing. It's true! It's a key phrase that you can use to get yourself and others to focus on the result you want to achieve, or the problem to be solved, instead of the confusion. You may also feel relieved that confusion isn't going to hang around like a fog that will haunt you forever. It's just something that's temporary. Defining confusion as a state of pre-clarity prevents you and others from devolving into a limiting story.

If people have a limiting story that says, "I'm confused" or its cousin "I'm overwhelmed," it puts the focus on the confusion and overwhelm rather than on the subject of the inquiry. What you want to do is put the focus on the question you're asking. Then you find clarity and space to think and reflect.

How do you help others find their commitment? Empowering people to find their own answers is more challenging than it might sound at first. In the urgency of life and business on a day-to-day basis, we often prefer to give someone an answer. Consider the idea that when you give a person a fish you feed them for a day. And when you teach a person to fish you feed them for a lifetime. Coaching people to fish rather than giving them a fish is why we guide them to their own answers, rather than giving them the answer. If I give you fish out of my freezer, which is full of fish, it takes about thirty seconds. If I teach you to fish, it takes longer; we have decisions to make. Is it ocean fishing ... lake fishing ... stream fishing? We have to talk about equipment, weather, and bait. But when you catch the fish, you're in action managing by your commitment.

Making a commitment is the bridge to getting things done. The funny thing is you usually don't have to make a commitment to what you're truly committed to. Have you ever noticed that? Golf, family, spiritual practice, yoga, tennis, running... all these come to mind! What you're already dedicated to, you do. Commitment builds a bridge to move you forward where you need a nudge in that direction ... from an idea of what you want, to having what you want. Not because others say so, but because you say so.

Practice: *Make sure your agreements are clear with yourself and others so you can manage by commitment.*

The challenge is not letting yourself "off the hook" of your commitments. You'll be glad you didn't. Think of the stories children tell of how their parents didn't push them to play piano and as adults they wish their parents had stood their ground. Stand your ground with your commitments. You already made the choice.

When you build a strong commitment born out of your vision, you bring inspiration and focus to the process of getting things done.

Chapter 27

The Voice Of Accountability

"It is not only what we do, but also what we do not do, for which we are accountable." Molière

Be accountable for the commitments you make and hold people to account for the promises they make to you. This is sometimes very challenging because it means confronting broken agreements. It means telling the truth.

I've seen and been told that what's missing from people telling the truth is a loving attitude. But what can also be missing from somebody who has a loving attitude is telling the truth! The truth is fundamental to being accountable and holding others accountable. Accountability means you are answerable, responsible for what you say and do.

Truth

I believe that what facilitates telling the truth is to speak with compassion. So, first, what do I mean by telling the truth? I think that your judgments or interpretations about what happened often masquerade as the truth. Truth is an accurate statement about the facts of the matter.

It's important to do some self-reflection here and ask yourself why you wouldn't tell someone the truth. In the workplace, some people tell me that they don't tell the truth because it wouldn't make a difference. I challenge that notion. If you don't tell the truth there's no opportunity for a real dialogue about what happened or what could change. And now I'm asking that you not only tell the truth, but you tell the truth with love. I use the word love because it jolts people awake to think about what communication would be like if it was actually possible to speak with love ... especially when love may be the furthest thing from your mind, let alone your heart.

Love

Love means that you are connected and present, interested in what someone is saying and what they see is possible. Love means goodwill, kindness, caring, and regard. You're not waiting for someone to fail, be embarrassed, feel guilty, humiliated, or give up. Love does not hide the truth or gloss over the truth. Love says, "I care enough to tell you the truth." Love also says, "I'm listening."

If love is too big a jump, think about a generosity of spirit and compassion toward yourself and others. I believe compassion comes when we recognize our humanity in each other. Just in living life day-to-day you notice that you've made mistakes and perhaps not recognized them until years later when you got some perspective. You most likely have let others or yourself down. I would guess that you also have experienced saying what's hard to say with anger, resentment, or frustration.

Accountability is an ethical concept meaning you are answerable and truthful.

When love and truth are the foundation of your voice

of accountability, you develop the capacity to see things as they are without adding fear. You can talk about the fact of what happened ... with interest. When fear is present, people are overly concerned about the outcome and are not present to be with the information in a way that can create a new idea, or solution; a lesson learned or forgiveness.

It helps to see love and truth as two sides of the same coin. Truth without love sounds like brutality. Someone may say something that hits the nail on the head, but we also feel that we've been hit on the head. Tennessee Williams, the playwright, said it best: "Cruel people always say they're just being frank." If you tell the truth with a hammer, all that people remember is the hammer. And it produces a culture of fear that can slow down people's willingness to speak up, take accountability, and be proactive and creative. Speaking the truth with love creates a culture of accountability. I think sometimes managers don't want to be loving because they're afraid they may have to fire someone or lay someone off later.

I find just the opposite is true. When you tell the truth with love people appreciate it. They know they can count on you not to mislead them. Be accountable and speak the truth or listen to the truth without being attached to a specific outcome. When you take accountability the answer is revealed.

I saw a billboard that read, "Be quick to listen and slow to speak." There is simple wisdom in that short sentence. Consider the setting for the truth. Some feedback is best done one-on-one, not in front of other people. At work if other people are involved you can brief the person in advance, and have them bring up an issue in the meeting. You're still holding them accountable, but you're allowing them to take responsibility. Rather than surprising them with corrective feedback in a meeting, let them know in advance so they can own up to the problem or the mistake and be in action to correct it. This creates ownership and is powerful. You don't need to hammer people with the truth, just tell them and coach them.

The other side of the equation of "truth and love" understands that love without truth is hypocrisy. How can you say, as a committed human being, as a coach, parent, or spouse that you genuinely care about a person or a company or the results and not tell the truth? You must be direct, clear, evenhanded, and give people the information they need, whether it's the good news or the bad news.

This has been part of an ongoing practice for me for many years, since I realized that one of my limiting stories included not hurting people's feelings. It hurts people more not to know the truth. When you speak the truth with love someone has the opportunity to respond. If your story is that you're waiting for the right time, look a little deeper and ask yourself why you're waiting. Withholding information can become a defeating habit. Blurting information is not the antidote. Telling the truth with love, with compassion, allows you to listen to someone's response and have a dialogue. Fulfillment is a practice that requires truth, love, and accountability.

Accountability does something important: it shifts your attention from finding someone to blame and focuses your attention on what you can do now. The voice of accountability is key in communication and is as important when you're dealing with your own accountability, as it is when you're dealing with others.

I've had many conversations with people about accountability and they'll ask, "Well, what if something happens that's really outside of your control? Or somebody else did something to you?" OK, let's say you're not accountable for what happened in those circumstances. You may still choose to keep looking for what you can learn versus defaulting to blame. Regardless of what happened in the past, how you respond now is your choice. Accountability allows you to have a conversation or make a new choice today, to create solutions that are unrelated to what you've done in the past. You use this attitude of accountability to give you a view of what can be done now, rather than to give you a hammer either to beat yourself up or bash other people. Accountability gives you power in the matter of what's occurring in your life today. Accountability allows you to see what is hidden when you're blaming yourself or others. It gives you insight and clarity. It gives you the ability to envision and create the future. Whenever I take accountability, even in the most difficult situations, I see solutions. I see what I can do, if I choose to. I prefer accountability because I don't want to be a victim of circumstances, conditions, or other people.

Several years ago I worked with an organization that had to lay off some people over a period of two months. This was a seasonal layoff in the hospitality industry. The manager spoke with his people and they came up with a solution. Rather than laying people off, everyone would take two week's vacation with no pay and reduce their hours; this way no one would be laid off and the company could cut expenses by the required amount. At first the corporate officers said no to this approach. I was coaching the president of the company and I asked him, "What are you looking for that their solution won't give you?" He couldn't answer. The associates' solution was timely and effective. As we continued to look at their solution he realized it gave something that his solution didn't. What it gave the company was the opportunity to keep the people he'd trained, knowing this was a temporary situation. He also realized he would gain something else—employee loyalty. All of these people were still with his organization several years later and no one had to be laid off. The employees took accountability and dealt with the issue. The employer listened. They all kept their commitments to each other and fulfillment was the result.

Accountability is hindered by fear and enhanced by kindness. When you can interrupt yourself or others in the act of limited thinking, speaking, or action, and take accountability, you're on your way to being fulfilled. You are present and connected not only with what is happening but with what is possible.

Practice: *Take accountability for your life just the way it is and just the way it isn't. Use this powerful practice to wake up and be present for what's available now.*

Accountability unlocks your power to change. Take accountability for your vision of a life worth living and start living it moment by moment, day by day, remembering that fulfillment is in the action you take right now.

Chapter 28

The Pull Of Completion

"The reward of a thing well done is to have done it!" Emerson

Now we'll talk about finishing what you set out to do. As discussed earlier completion is key to fulfillment. Let's review before I invite you to take the challenge.

If you are having a hard time knowing your vision of a life worth living, discovering your original promise, and setting fulfilling goals, ask yourself whether there's anything that is incomplete.

When people are incomplete they carry their unfinished projects, relationships, and conversations around like a burden. What's incomplete can be distracting and it will consume energy. If you have a lot of loose ends, it may be difficult for you to visualize taking on anything new, let alone a vision of a life worth living!

I was coaching an individual who was having a hard time considering what would be fulfilling for her. So I asked, "Is there anything that is incomplete?" She laughed and waved her arms and said, "Are you kidding?" However, I continued in earnest to explore this area. Once we started looking it was clear that she had made many promises and hadn't completed them, and most of these promises she made to herself. She no longer trusted herself to keep her word. She didn't want to set any new goals or consider the possibility that she could both fulfill new results and be happy along the way.

So we took the step-by-step approach and set up a process where she wrote down all the things she had promised to do but hadn't completed. I asked her to put everything on the list, without concern about whether she was actually going to do it or not. The list consisted of everything from books she said she would read that were still sitting on the table next to her bed, to the tax returns she hadn't sent in for two years, to conversations she told herself she would have but never took the time to actually have them. You can be incomplete with people as well as with things. This was a truth-telling process not a self-judgment process. If you start to judge yourself for why you did or didn't do something earlier you may find yourself back in self-limiting stories, spinning the wheels of your mind, rather than just making the list and getting clarity on what needs to be done ... if anything.

Remember the way you'll know you're still incomplete? You'll talk to yourself continually about what happened, what you need to do, or what you should have done or said.

Completion Is A Process

To get started in this completion process, I asked her to review her list and do one of four things:

1. Delete the promise if it was to herself and she wasn't going to do it.

2. Revoke her promise if she made the promise to another person and she wasn't going to do it now or in the future. Tell the other person the truth. Make the phone call.

3. Make clear goals to complete. Write down the strategy, action steps, and a time frame. Make the commitment and then do it!

4. Define what would be appropriate to put in a tickler file and review in a specific time frame. (I didn't want that file to become a storehouse of unfinished business. What got in her tickler file were things she truly wanted to do but in a future time frame, in one year. They weren't really incomplete; they were aspirations for the future.)

Now here's what happened: The two-year unpaid taxes got handled within thirty days. And every other item on the list was completed within sixty days, including those incomplete conversations. Those were hard! There are consequences to revoking your promises and there also are great gains in telling the truth and saying no. There may be short term angst but the freedom you experience and the opportunity to create a relationship that works makes it worthwhile. I was a rigorous fulfillment coach with every promise she made, and she checked in once a week with a progress report. I watched the energy of this person change from limitation to freedom, a freedom to take action and a freedom to reinvent herself as a successful person. Finishing is the key to being successful and fulfilled. As a result of this process she was ready to take on some life-changing goals. She had rebuilt trust in her own word.

You can take action to be complete. If you decide you are not going to complete a commitment that you made, ask yourself what changed since you set the goal. What's different today from when you started?

If you decide to complete it you may find yourself ending an old limiting story. You'll see a shift in your performance and in who you are as a fulfilled human being in the simple act of finishing.

If you keep talking to yourself about some specific idea that's incomplete, and you know you're not going to do it now but it still interests you, put it on hold for a period of time and then review it. Create your own tickler file with a specific date to review. It may be kindling to ignite a new vision

In business, managers have a unique opportunity; they can be fulfillment coaches for their people. They also have the opportunity to see their own supervisors as coaches. In this way a culture of fulfillment is established by how you speak, listen, and act. And by the results you achieve.

Practice: *Continue the practice of saying at the end of each day, "I am complete for today." If there's something that intrudes on your statement, schedule the action.*

Be your word and do what you say. You can't force other people to complete, nor can you do it for them. If someone is incomplete with you, call the person and have a completion conversation. If that's not possible, learn the lesson and let it go.

Completion is a powerful meditation on carefully considering promises before you make them or accept them ... a wake-up call in the practice of fulfillment.

Chapter 29

The Mirror Of Relationship

"One cannot be strong without love. For love is not an irrelevant emotion; it is the blood of life, the power of reunion of the separated." Paul Tillich

It was many years ago that my husband and I developed a program called *On Course: A Journey Home* that was dedicated to having individuals recognize their connection with all of life and be present to experience it. This program brought a deep sense of the background of relationship available when we operate from connection, and contrarily what happens when we operate from separation in our thoughts, words, and actions.

It's ironic when we are close with another human being and then something unexpected happens. Maybe it's a difference of opinion, conflict, disagreement, and then we "see" that person differently. We see them through the eyes of separation ... no longer friend but enemy. Can we have conflict, differences, and disagreement from connection and have our relationships not only weather the storm, but get stronger?

You'll hear the difference in people's conversation when they're operating from connection rather than separation. If the connection remains you'll hear people say things like, "We agreed to disagree. We have a difference of opinion in this matter. I don't agree and they do have a point. We're learning from each other and from what happened. We're growing!" When it's coming from separation you'll hear things like "They don't have the right to exist. They're jerks. I'm right and they're wrong. How could they do this to me?" You can ask, "What happened?" from connection, take accountability and self-correct. You can ask the same question from separation, blame the other person and chalk it up to another disappointment.

I actually finished this book without a specific chapter on relationships, but the notion of being fulfilled without looking into the nature of relationship kept calling me to put pen to paper and continue the exploration.

Relationships can be so fulfilling and oh ... so disappointing. Relationships require that you face yourself. True relationships are like mirrors—they reflect back to you aspects of yourself that might otherwise stay hidden. If you experience the same thing over and over in relationship you may begin to notice the common denominator is you, and it's time to look a little deeper into how you are being in relationship.

The Fulfillment In Relationship

What is the fulfillment in relationship? I believe the fulfillment in relationship is you wanting to be where you are whether it's in a conversation, sharing a meal, participating in a meeting, working in a job or in bed! It's the expression of connection and presence.

The practice of connection and presence allows you to bring your attention and awareness to this moment right now. It opens you up to be who you are and grants that same opening to another. What an amazing gift to give to another human being that around you, they can be authentic, they can be themselves.

True relationship is the result of this practice of

connection and presence. Connection is the link between you and another. The link can actually be forged through challenges and conflict by solving problems together. The link is also forged through understanding that opinions are not a substitute for truth and agreements aren't automatic. Shared interests and vision forge the link, but just as important is the support for those exciting differences in tastes, desires, and passions.

Relationships can be strengthened or weakened over time but the link still exists. Have you ever noticed when you see an old friend who you haven't seen for years and in the moment of being together again it was like no time had passed? You catch up, laugh, and are enriched by knowing each other. The connection is felt and acknowledged. What happens with that old friend if conflicts or feelings are unresolved? The connection is still there. You may notice however that what you're connected to are the unresolved feelings instead of the relationship, as it exists today.

It seems to me that the past doesn't get integrated until you learn the lessons that the relationship can teach you. The fulfillment in relationship is learning, waking up, and knowing yourself and others more fully and intimately. It's hard to integrate losing, failure, or painful experiences, but it's essential to being aware and it's essential to growing in relationship.

It may be challenging for you to see the connection with difficult people, antagonistic situations, past hurts, or an undesired state of mind. Pretending that you're separate from these states is like trying to cut off a piece of yourself instead of just being with it. And yet, if you can just notice it, like connecting with an old friend, you can see it as it is now and remain open to learning any undiscovered lessons. Then you can let the past go.

It helps to remind yourself that life isn't perfect, relationships aren't perfect, and you're not perfect. Perfection is an ideal that at some point you can trade in for a real and authentic relationship with yourself and others.

Instead of looking for what's missing in the other person, start by finding that missing quality inside yourself and in your expression. If honesty is missing, be honest. If listening is missing, listen. If peace at all costs is your strategy, try a little honesty even if it means you argue. A little peaceful arguing lets other people know how you feel about something.

I am blessed to have many loving relationships and we are all free to say what we think. We argue about politics, the meaning of life, spirituality, exercise, the environment, business, and global warming. We argue in the true meaning of the word, to give reasons and evidence in support of an idea. We learn from our arguments. There's no intention to silence the other person's voice. In fact on some occasions, we do argue to persuade each other and each of us is left better informed, more understanding of the different ideas, and we regularly find common ground. Why is this possible? Love is the language of connection and presence. Instead of attachment to ideas, we extend a generosity of spirit. We're more interested in mining the depths of each other than coming to a conclusion.

It's to the detriment of our world not to acknowledge that we're all in this together. While you may not agree with another person, religion, or nation, it doesn't change the fact that we all are connected.

The practice of being connected and present challenges our ability to be with another person fully available with our heart and mind. It's so easy to get distracted by jobs, business, family, concerns, the news, finances, and the assorted commitments we have in our daily lives. We don't often take the time just to be with people we love. To stop what we're doing and look into their eyes and say, "I love you." Even rarer is stopping to look into the eyes of people we see every day at work and connect with who they are and be present to listen unconditionally.

Practice: *Start where you are in the practice of connection and presence. Think about what you're connected to. Is it the person you're talking to or your idea about the person?*

Start with your family and the people you work with. Take a breath and silently tell yourself before a conversation, "I am one with you. I am here now." Our shorthand way of making these statements is the mantra, "one-now." Invoke it often as a silent affirmation. It will open up conversations about ideas, what happened, possibilities, and solutions. It will engage you in your relationships to tell the truth with compassion.

Practicing one-now is practical and deeply fulfilling. It ends the illusion of separation. It allows dialogue and discussion as a replacement for the reactive mind. It allows you to be more committed to resolution than being right. It allows you to forgive and let go. It allows you to learn and grow. It brings you into the mystery of love ... a treasure that accelerates awareness and growth in the true meaning of relationship—the state of being connected and present.

Chapter 30

Fulfillment Practices – Accept The Challenge

"Happiness is when what you think, what you say, and what you do are in harmony." Mahatma Gandhi

Remember the story of the master of Kyudo who when asked how long it took him to become a master said, "Do you mean how long did it take before I learned that all there is, is practice?" I still laugh when I think of the story. I also recognize the truth in the statement. I carry that truth in my practices. For me it's a statement about fulfillment. There's nowhere to get to. If fulfillment isn't here and now, it's nowhere. Fulfillment isn't some past missed opportunity or idealized future fantasy; it's available in this present moment, in your practice. The promise of fulfillment is in your thoughts, words, and actions.

I believe in these three magic words … practice makes progress. With practice you can learn anything and be successful. Practice demonstrates commitment; it shows dedication and follow-through.

The Challenge

Apply these practices in the areas that are most challenging for you. If it's finding your vision of a life worth living, start there. If it's in relationship, start there. If you have a conflict, start there. If you're unhappy in your job, start there. Apply these practices to open up your thinking and actions with the most difficult person or the most difficult situation where fulfillment seems elusive. Apply these practices to that person or situation first, and see what kind of difference you can make. It will give you ownership of these skills, give you a place to practice, and leave you in action to be fulfilled now.

I don't divide the world up into committed people and uncommitted people. I think we can safely say that everyone is committed. They're committed to something. Use this book to find out what you're committed to. If you continue to be committed to the story that something can't be done, ask yourself how that story serves you today. Does it serve your vision of a life that matters ... to you?

Some people say life is too short to wait to be fulfilled. I say life is too long to do what's not fulfilling. It may be time for you to generate for yourself that your life matters; your vision of a life worth living is possible. Once you heed that call, make a plan and do it. Time passes whether you do anything or not. You'll wake up four years from now and wonder why you didn't get started. Wonder now and get started now. It's never too late. I've said it several times in this book; progress is not automatic. Progress is a series of steps you take that move you in the direction you want to go, reminding you that the results you seek are possible.

Fulfillment Practices

The ideas in this book are meant to stimulate fulfillment practices that will keep you on course both to accomplish your goals and to grow in awareness. They are designed for you to experience fulfillment on the way to fulfilling your goals. They are simple and effective. They will inform you. They will instill in you the understanding that you are more than what you do. These fulfillment practices are designed to reconcile who you are with what you do in the world.

1. **Listen To What You Say.**
   Be vigilant and listen to what you say to yourself and others. What you say speaks volumes about what you think is possible and what you think limits you. Your words give you an inside track to notice what you really believe. Your words are declarative and shape reality. Just notice and if your words lead you away from fulfillment—or sound like a self-limiting story—stop and take it back. Say something like, "Hmmm that's an old story." Even if it has been true, it's only true up until now.

2. **Declare What You Want Instead Of What You Don't Want.**
   Notice whether deciding what you don't want is leading you closer to knowing what you want. Practice following any statement about what you don't want with a statement about what you do want, or a statement about your vision or what ignites your passion. It could be as simple as saying, "I don't want to go out to dinner tonight. I want to stay home and cook." Begin to trace what you want back to your vision of a life worth living.

3. **Let Your Vision Of A Life Worth Living Guide And Organize Your Actions.**
   A new vision is often born out of something that is missing for you personally or in your community, your business, or the world. A vision aligned with your original promise changes you and the world you live in. When you take actions that leave you with a limiting

story or excuses about why you did what you did, use the story as a flashlight to examine the conditions you give in to that don't support your vision.

4. **Write Down What You Want To Accomplish.**
   When you write down your goals also write down why that particular goal would give meaning to your life. Align your goals with your passion, your vision of a life worth living, your original promise. Writing down your vision and goals brings focus and awareness to your actions. What you focus on prospers.

5. **Take Actions That Focus On Fulfillment.**
   This is what you say is important. Avoid activities that are not important! Quietly stop before each action and ask yourself this fulfillment question, "Will the action I'm taking sustain fulfillment through tomorrow?" Create fulfillment in the action you take right now, in the choices you're making right now. You'll know it's a fulfilling action because you won't have a conversation about what you did or didn't do tomorrow! Use the fulfillment question as part of your daily practice when you're making choices about what to do. Slowing down the moment between desire and action holds great power—the power of conscious choice. If your answer to the question "Will my action sustain fulfillment through tomorrow?" is "Hmmm ... probably not," most likely it's an activity that fills up your time but not your health, wealth, or happiness.

6. **Turn Your Complaints Into Well-Aimed Requests.**
   Think through the requests you can make that will forward your goals. Determine who is the most

appropriate person to ask. Who could actually consider, and has the ability, to fulfill your request? This practice takes courage and will change your life. It will cause you to think through what you want to make happen. Use it wisely and if you're not going to make a request or do something about the nature of your complaint, stop complaining! You will free up your time and create space for new thinking.

7. **Stop Waiting And Start Now.**
   You can only start where you are. The truth is you can't start anywhere else. Time will pass whether you start or not. Thinking you should have started earlier only postpones getting to the beginning line. All achievements start with that first step. What is a risk worth taking? Most often you have to risk awkwardness, embarrassment, what other people think, and the possibility of failure.

   I've had people tell me that attachment to their image (the possibility of being embarrassed) prevents them from risking a new behavior or even having a truthful conversation about what they think. While most people will say they are open to new ideas, learning new skills, and new ways of being, in practice they are only open to the "known". The known is what they already agree with, what they've already learned or where they're already proven. Your vision may move you into the unknown. When you stop waiting and start now in the direction of your vision, what you have to gain is fulfillment, learning, freedom, and achievement.

8. **Take 100% Accountability.**
   Remember that blaming yourself, conditions, or others
   for what is happening doesn't forward new solutions.
   Recognition of "what is" allows you to cross the gap
   between the way it is and the way you think it should be
   and ask what's possible now. Reaction and defensiveness
   widens the gap. Suspending reaction allows you to be
   fully present to deal with what is showing up today.

   100% accountability says there is something you can do.
   Use the practice of 100% accountability to give you a
   view into what happened, what you can learn and what's
   possible now just as it is. This includes asking for help
   when you need it, taking action that makes a difference
   and the peace of mind that comes from knowing you've
   done all you can do.

9. **Let Go Of Attachment To The Outcome.**
   Attachment is not focus. Attachment is fear. When you
   let go you can listen, be present, deal with obstacles,
   and receive feedback to refine or correct your course of
   action. Non-attachment lets you start at the beginning
   and stay there until you develop proficiency. How do
   you know you're attached? One sure-fire way to notice is
   you stop listening. Or you'll notice that there's only one
   way, your way. You may be acting out of emotion: anger,
   frustration, or complaining about people who just don't
   get "it" or perhaps your attachment comes across as
   silent irritation.

   Letting go of attachment to an outcome, while
   maintaining a high level of participation, allows you
   to see what's missing. It takes off the blinders that only

allow you to see one way or the "right" way while missing key opportunities, resources, and relationships. Letting go of attachment brings your focus back to now. Instead of attachment, operate from a spirit of inquiry and let the practice of discovery inform you and your goals.

10. **Tell The Truth With Love.**
Let your words be truthful, thoughtful, and generous. Allow for silence. It's an indication that others are being with their thoughts. This may require slowing down if your words come from reaction rather than a thoughtful response. If your habit is to not speak up, this practice may be made easier if you start with a declarative statement like, "I have something to say." Then say it. If your habit is to interrupt or fill up every silence with words, ask yourself why you feel the need to interrupt. In conversations when you catch yourself interrupting, just acknowledge the interruption and then listen.

When you tell the truth be prepared to listen. Telling the truth with love is an exchange. The underlying practice is to listen with love. Love allows for differences and leaves people whole. Love acknowledges connection. Love brings you present so you can talk about anything.

11. **Say Thank You To Feedback.**
You can say thank you whether you initially agree or don't agree with the feedback. Saying thank you allows you to listen and consider the feedback. Feedback is natural in the process of accomplishing anything. Your body gives you feedback when you exercise. Your boss gives you feedback on performance. Your actions give

you feedback on what works and what doesn't work. Listen to feedback as an opening to learn something new and make any necessary course corrections in your thoughts, words, or actions.

12. **Be Your Word.**

Carefully consider what you say yes to. Deliver on what you promise, understanding that your promises create a pledge. They're not conditional unless the conditions are made clear at the beginning. If there are conditions to your promises, make them explicit. There will be less clean up, incomplete plans, and ongoing conversations about why you didn't do it!

13. **Say No.**

Saying no is the beginning of authentic choice. I know someone who said no to every request. She found it was easier to later change a no into a yes than a yes into a no. It was in this way she stopped being an automatic "yes machine".

No is a promise and makes choice possible. No is a promise not to do something now. Say no with a smile and if you're worried that you won't be considered in the future, make a request to be considered next time!

14. **Never Give Up.**

Keep learning. A course of action or a strategy may fail; it's life, growth, and continuous learning. You are not your strategies; who you are is borne out by the example of your life, the promises you make, and the love you give.

15. **Enjoy Yourself!**

I had a necklace with a charm that had three words: live, love, laugh. This is a great reminder in the everyday living of our lives. In the search for fulfillment remember to live, love, and laugh ... and you will find that you are fulfilled along the way.

These practices may be the beginning of an examined life or for some, a lifelong continuation of a discussion about accomplishment and awareness; about life and why we're here.

Fulfillment for all of us is a radically different way to see and operate in the world. You don't operate one way in your personal life and another way at work. You don't live a divided life. Your original promise, your calling, transcends what you want and what you don't want. It is you, the expression and recognition of who you are. The pull to reconcile who you are with what you do becomes stronger. Insights will come, life courses will alter, and the realization will dawn that you are waking up from the trance of existence to start living by your own design. Begin now.

Epilogue

In December of 2005, my husband Michael, our friend Wally, and I decided to go on a writers' retreat in Santa Barbara. It wasn't a formal retreat conducted by authors or teachers, but we dubbed it a writers' retreat because all of us talk and write as part of our work. We could have called it a vision quest but it had more in common with an Algonquin Round Table experience than a vision quest, since there were no purifying rituals, meditations, or silent walks. It was a time where each of us could reflect on our vision of a life worth living and the impact we could have in our families, at work and in the world. We all began to look at the direction our life's journey was taking us.

We spent long mornings walking the winding road down to Pierre Lafond's for coffee, sharing our thoughts, laughing at each other's stories, and then would return to our rooms at the rustic retreat center at La Casa de Maria to write down our ideas. Three days later Wally returned to Los Angeles and Michael and I headed to Northern California where we live.

Like returning from a great vacation, the feeling of contentment stayed with me for a short period of time, but the idea of writing as a way to contact and lift people's spirits remained unshakable. My approach to doing most things is simply to start and learn as I go. For me the commitment comes right on the heels of a vision. This project would challenge everything I knew. I was clear on the vision, to give my readers tools they can use to deal with the challenges of their lives and leave them in action to live their idea of fulfillment.

And so I began. I started with revisiting and writing

about my tried and tested work with people, conducted over years of training and management. I know that vision without action is a fantasy. Still, a true vision is a calling and works in mysterious and surprising ways. I quickly noticed that the universe was attracting the people I needed to help me on this great adventure and put me on the path to completion. My daughter moved to Northern California and asked to read my manuscript. She was a LA girl, working in the fast-paced, high energy, intense city environment of the home entertainment industry. It was one thing to write in the privacy of my thoughts. It was just me and my computer, scraps of papers, journals, and google. It was talking about ideas and titles with my husband. My daughter has a way of insisting ... with love. She takes after me. So I gave her the manuscript. She promptly sat me down, reworked the organization of the book, put me on a schedule, and found an editor. I look back at that time and laugh. It was when I knew I would finish.

I take to heart the idea that "Until one is committed, there is hesitancy, the chance to draw back. Concerning all acts of initiative (and creation), there is one elementary truth, the ignorance of which kills countless ideas and splendid plans: *that the moment one definitely commits oneself, then Providence moves too.* All sorts of things occur to help one that would never otherwise have occurred. A whole stream of events issues from the decision, raising in one's favor all manner of unforeseen incidents and meetings and material assistance, which no one could have dreamed would ... come. Whatever you can do, or dream you can do, begin it. Boldness has genius, power, and magic in it. Begin it now."

Although this quote has been widely contributed to Goethe, it's actually from a mountain climber by the name of W. H. Murray who acknowledged Goethe as the author of the last two lines. According to the Goethe Society, Goethe actually said, "Boldness has genius, power, and magic in it. Only engage, and then the mind grows heated. Begin it, and the work will be completed." That works for me!

You'll find that fulfillment is your natural state and comes in many forms, from a stranger smiling unexpectedly, the smell of bread baking, laughter among friends, telling the truth with compassion, discovering shared interests, resolving old conflicts, as well as accomplishing a life goal. Don't put off the things that matter most to you. Engage now and what you dream about will come forward. The years go by whether you do anything or not. It matters little, at this point in time, that you haven't already done it. You can't go back and change what you did or didn't do yesterday, but you can start now.

My encouragement goes with you.

Recommended Reading

I'm a voracious reader. I love books that transport me to a different world of ideas. I remember being told that geniuses are people who can create a world and get other people to live in it with them. That's the domain of authors and leaders I admire most, whether I'm reading a book, a newspaper article (yes, I still read the newspaper), or listening to conversations that send a wake-up call to some part of me that's been asleep. While I'm reading, I live in the world the author creates and am inspired to think about the mysteries of human behavior; why we do what we do, and most importantly, to contemplate how we can impact beneficial and useful change, in the midst of living busy and full lives.

Quotes To Ponder

The following are some of my favorite quotes that didn't make it into the chapters, for your enjoyment and inspiration:

"I've learned ... everyone wants to live on top of the mountain, but all the happiness and growth occurs while you're climbing it." Andy Rooney

"I wish I had worked to change the framework, rather than to work within that framework." Timothy Geithner regarding the New York Fed

"Action toward goals, other than happiness, (is what) makes us happy. Though there is a place for vegging out and reading trashy novels, easy pleasures will never light us up the way mastering a new skill or building something from scratch will." Carlin Flora in Psychology Today on The Pursuit of Happiness

"The CEO's who are most likely to succeed are humble, diffident relentless, and a bit unidimensional. They are often not the most exciting people to be around." David Brooks commenting on a study called Which CEO Characteristics and Abilities Matter?

"We cannot put off living until we are ready. The most salient characteristic of life is its coerciveness; it is always urgent, here and now, without any possible postponement." José Ortega Y. Gasset

"Love is the strangest thing that I know, you keep it around by letting it go." Michael Sun

"Keep knocking and the joy inside will eventually open a window and look to see who's there." Rumi

"I want to be the architect of my own embarrassment." Mike Myers

"Change is inevitable. Change for the better is a full time job." Adlai Stevenson

"I go to bed at one a.m. and get up at five. I don't like the first five minutes, but that's life ... Is it better to be sleeping or better to be up getting another two hours of real-life drama? You say you get up at seven. So you miss two hours a day, seven days a week, 365 days a year. That's a major hit. Most people work 8 hours per day. Two more hours is 25% extra. That's like living until you are 80 instead of 64." Dennis Conner, Sailor

"Make it so." Captain Jean-Luc Picard

Books To Read

The following are a few of the books I'd recommend that give insights into the subject of fulfillment.

Ending The Pursuit Of Happiness: A Zen Guide by Barry Magid; published by Wisdom Publications

The Geography Of Bliss by Eric Weiner; published by the Hachette Book Group

Eat, Pray, Love by Elizabeth Gilbert; published by the Penguin Group

Getting To Yes by Roger Fisher and William Ury; published by the Penguin Group

The Tao Of Leadership by John Heider; published by Bantum Books

Finite and Infinte Games: A Vision of Life as Play and Possibility by James P. Carse; published by The Ballantine Publishing Group

Lord Of The Rings by J.R.R. Tolkien; published by Houghton Mifflin

A New Earth, Awakening To Your Life's Purpose by Eckhart Tolle; published by the Penguin Group

Stumbling on Happiness by Daniel Gilbert; published by Alfred A. Knopf

A Simple Path by The Dalai Lama; published by

Thorsons, Harper Collins

The Wisdom of Insecurity by Alan Watts; published by Knopf Doubleday Publishing Group

The Feminine Mystique by Betty Friedan; published by Dell Publishing

Priceless, Turning Ordinary Products into Extraordinary Experiences by Diana LaSalle and Terry A. Britton; published by Harvard Business School Publishing

The Audacity of Hope by Barack Obama; published by Three Rivers Press, a division of Random House

Yoga Beyond Belief: Insights to Awaken and Deepen Your Practice by Ganga White; published by North Atlantic Books

About The Author

Paulette has worked with thousands of people as a trainer, coach, and business leader. She is the CEO of *one-now*, a division of Empowerment Technology Corporation. She teaches that the power to change awakens when you have the courage to envision what's possible, and take the necessary actions to make it happen.

Paulette lives in Northern California with her husband. She runs half-marathons and is working on her next book.

You can contact Paulette at www.one-now.com

LaVergne, TN USA
23 July 2010
190641LV00002B/2/P

9 780578 016450